More Praise for <u>Leading Geeks</u>

"Paul Glen masterfully and humorously teaches us how to create followership in this notoriously inscrutable but essential population. Ignore his rock-solid advice at your own peril."

—Andrew Sobel, author, *Clients for Life* and *Making Rain*

"*Leading Geeks* nails the complex geek psyche and offers pragmatic advice and insight for those who wish to harness the power of these most valuable employees. This book is required reading for anyone in my company who works with geeks."

—Michael Mori, president, Network Insight

"Paul Glen has put a lot of thought into the particular (and at times peculiar) needs of the technical computer staff—the geeks. For those who must lead technical personnel, this book offers some invaluable 'aha's' regarding what makes them tick and how to capitalize on their idiosyncrasies to achieve outstanding performance. And Glen doesn't stop there. Even if you're a seasoned technical manager, you can't get through this book without picking up a few tips to make your job easier and your group more effective."

—Jeff Chasney, senior vice president and chief information officer, Carl Karcher Enterprises

"This book is a must-read for anyone who has to deal with the techno-geeks of today's society. Paul has encapsulated the essence of managing these folks effectively without losing his sense of humor and his perspective."

—Marsha Lewin, author, *The Overnight Consultant*, *The Consultant's Survival Guide*, *Better Software Project Management*, and coauthor, *Software Project Management*

"*Leading Geeks* provides a unique and pragmatic perspective on the issues faced by technologists as they create value within an organization. The ideas here will help any technical business."

—Allen Dickason, senior vice president and chief technology officer, Kinko's

"I recognize the geeks Mr. Glen describes from my time at Apple Computer working with the team that invented the Macintosh. If I'd had this book in 1981, there's no doubt that I could have better served the human resources needs of that team."

—Vicki Milledge, program manager, emerging leaders program, Center for Collaborative Leadership, University of Massachusetts Boston

"This book is a must-read for all who struggle with leading the technical workforce. I'm going to be assigning it to all my students."

—David Finegold, head of strategy and organizations studies, Keck Graduate Institute for Applied Life Sciences

"This book is a great read, easily understood and logically organized. It will definitely help leaders gain the skills needed to be successful in today's technologically dependent organizations."

—Ronne Froman, rear admiral, United States Navy (retired)

"Although ostensibly about technologists, *Leading Geeks* provides broader insights into the nature and management of knowledge workers in general. In fact, this book would be very valuable for university managers who are trying to 'lead' their faculty knowledge workers!"

—Margaret Hellie Huyck, professor of psychology, Illinois Institute of Technology

"Using gentle humor and keen intellect, Paul Glen pries the covers off an often mysterious group of key contributors. Wondering what makes geeks tick, and how to get them ticking in sync with the rest of the business? This book will show you how."

—Marian Cook, president, Ageos Enterprises

Warren Bennis

A WARREN BENNIS BOOK

This collection of books is devoted exclusively to new and exemplary contributions to management thought and practice. The books in this series are addressed to thoughtful leaders, executives, and managers of all organizations who are struggling with and committed to responsible change. My hope and goal is to spark new intellectual capital by sharing ideas positioned at an angle to conventional thought—in short, to publish books that disturb the present in the service of a better future.

Books in the Warren Bennis Signature Series

Branden
Self-Esteem at Work

Mitroff, Denton
A Spiritual Audit of Corporate America

Schein
The Corporate Culture Survival Guide

Sample
The Contrarian's Guide to Leadership

Lawrence, Nohria
Driven

Cloke, Goldsmith
*The End of Management and the
Rise of Organizational Democracy*

Glen
Leading Geeks

Leading Geeks

Leading Geeks

How to Manage and Lead People Who Deliver Technology

Paul Glen

Foreword by
David H. Maister

JOSSEY-BASS
A Wiley Imprint
www.josseybass.com

Published by Jossey-Bass
A Wiley Imprint
989 Market Street, San Francisco, CA 94103-1741   www.josseybass.com

Jossey-Bass books and products are available through most bookstores. To contact Jossey-Bass directly call our Customer Care Department within the U.S. at 800-956-7739, outside the U.S. at 317-572-3986 or fax 317-572-4002.

Jossey-Bass also publishes its books in a variety of electronic formats. Some content that appears in print may not be available in electronic books.

Library of Congress Cataloging-in-Publication Data

Glen, Paul, 1965-
 Leading geeks: how to manage and lead people who deliver technology /
Paul Glen; foreword by David H. Maister.
    p. cm.
"A Warren Bennis book."
Includes bibliographical references and index.
 ISBN 0-7879-6148-5 (alk. paper)
 1. Technology-Management. I. Title.
 T49.5. G554 2003
 658.5'7—dc21   2002011845

Printed in the United States of America
FIRST EDITION
HB Printing   10 9 8 7 6 5 4 3 2 1

Contents

Editor's Note

Every day, new technology is revolutionizing the way we work and the way we live. Companies and leaders unwilling or unable to embrace technology have watched their more adaptable competitors pass them by. Meanwhile, top technology workers are in high demand, which has allowed to persist the idea that eccentric, unmanageable "geeks" must be accepted as a necessary evil. When conventional leadership methods fail to work with geeks, many managers throw up their hands because "that's just the way it is."

With so much riding on the timely and skillful deployment of new technologies, leaders can't get by merely tolerating geeks; they must find new ways to motivate and manage them to maximize the value of their work. Paul Glen has been on both sides of the fence, as a self-proclaimed geek and as a geek leader. There's no guesswork here—he knows the people, he knows how they think and how they work, he's been one of them. *Leading Geeks* gets inside the heads of technology workers and clearly explains what drives them to excel. The very nature of geeks—their love of challenge and their desire to create solutions—presents a vast and largely untapped resource for organizations. Glen's insights and experience provide the keys to unlocking this potential.

This book is exactly the blueprint that leaders of technology workers need; it describes the obstacles they face and provides solid solutions. Glen illustrates the best methods for motivating geeks, using their talents most effectively, and bridging the communication gap between geeks and the rest of the organization. *Leading Geeks* is also a guide to attracting and keeping the best technology talent. Geeks don't bestow their loyalty on a leader for the same reasons that other employees do, nor are they easily won over by the video games and other perks of dot-com lore. The leader who understands and respects the geek way of life will reap far greater benefit than one who throws money at the problem. As Glen points out, geek loyalty is elusive but is staunch once achieved.

For leaders of organizations around the world, the Technology Revolution has been the type of event that Robert J. Thomas and I, in our book *Geeks and Geezers*, describe as a "crucible." Whether you pass the test is up to you; by holding this book in your hands, you are already well on your way.

Santa Monica, California   WARREN BENNIS
September 2002

Foreword

In this important and useful book, Paul Glen tackles a frontier topic in business, and does so in a way that makes a significant contribution to our understanding not only of geeks, but of professional people in general.

His articulation of the manager's tasks (provide internal facilitation, manage ambiguity, nurture motivation, and furnish external representation) is an innovative and insightful contribution to what real-world managers must do and how they serve their teams. Glen's years of practical experience are clearly reflected in the text and make this book a practical guide to action that will provide managers of technical professionals (inside corporations or in service provider firms) with concrete suggestions and, perhaps as valuable, new ways of thinking. Rather than recycle conventional thinking, he offers his own stimulating thoughts. Experienced managers as well as neophytes will find something here for them.

The book will also be of value to those who hire and deal with technical teams or interact with them in other ways, such as the venture capitalists and other financiers who must decide whether to fund technical enterprises. The old phrase "knowledge is power" is not quite correct. *Understanding* is power, and that's what Glen provides.

It is important to note that much of what is written about management and leadership attempts to be universal, providing lessons

drawn from diverse contexts and organizations with diverse objectives. In other work, we have been invited to consider the leadership secrets of military, political, royal, and religious leaders, as well
as leaders of businesses of all kinds, from industrial to retail to consumer service industries.

Glen, appropriately, rejects this universalist approach. His careful analysis of the special characteristics of technical work, the individuals who choose to do that work, how they function in groups,
and what all this implies for how they can be managed is a framework that others could productively follow.

While his focus is on geeks, much of what Glen has to say par-
allels the situation of other professional settings. I recommend this
book to those who must lead other knowledge workers in a wide
variety of professional settings. The book raises fascinating questions about what skills managers should possess and how they
should be selected.

The test of any worthwhile book is that it forces you to stop
reading and consider what the author has said. *Leading Geeks* passes
this test repeatedly. While its style is breezy and accessible enough
to allow a quick read, it is filled with challenging assertions that
contain myriads of implications. Glen doesn't hedge his views: he
states them boldly. You don't have to accept all of these views to be
forced to think, "I wonder if he's right? If he is, then what follows
from that?" No author can provide the reader with greater value.

Boston, Massachusetts   DAVID H. MAISTER
September 2002

Introduction

You can't live with 'em and you can't live without 'em. No, I'm not talking about the opposite sex. I'm talking about geeks, a.k.a. nerds, computer jockeys, or knowledge workers—the people who design, build, test, install, and support computer technology from mighty mainframes in their climate-controlled glass citadels to the humble PCs on every desktop. In the knowledge-driven, hyper-competitive, 24-7 economy, geeks are a key weapon in a business's arsenal. As technology continues to drive business productivity and competitiveness, the role of the geek becomes increasingly critical. Some think that whichever organization attracts and retains the best geeks wins in this environment. They're only half right.

Just getting the best geeks isn't good enough. You've got to know what to do with them. Even the most intelligent, motivated, good-willed geeks don't always succeed. Just think about all those dead dot-coms.

Success requires not just having good geeks, but leading them. And with technology infiltrating every area of business, from sales and marketing to operations and human resources, all managers must learn to lead geeks.

Geeks are notoriously difficult to manage and lead. Their work is frequently difficult to understand. Their demands for funds often seem insatiable. Their deliverables are always late. And, perhaps most frustrating of all, they don't respond to traditional methods of command and control.

So where do you turn? Unfortunately, most books on leadership won't be much help. In fact, much of what you already know about leadership won't work with geeks for three primary reasons:

1. *Geeks are different from other employees.* (You probably figured out this one in grammar school.) Most leadership books begin with the fundamental assumption that leadership is a relationship between leaders and followers, and then proceed to focus almost exclusively on the knowledge, attitudes, beliefs, ethics, and behaviors of the leader, as if the nature of followers were irrelevant. But as most of you already know, not all followers are alike, and they do not respond to leadership in the same way. Geeks in particular are a special group requiring different care and feeding from others in an organization.

2. *Geekwork, the intricate, technological knowledge work that geeks perform, is different from other types of work.* Most discussions of leadership assume that leading a group of first graders on a field trip to a museum is the same as guiding a nation into war. Of course, this simply isn't true. What you are trying to lead people to do does, in fact, affect the nature of the relationship between leaders and followers.

3. *Power, the basis of most approaches to leadership, is relatively useless when dealing with geeks.* It's not just that they can be recalcitrant (which they often are), but that the nature of power renders it . . . well . . . powerless. Power is the ability to effect the behavior of others, but geeks don't deliver value through behavior. They deliver value mostly through thought rather than action, so their behavior has relatively little effect on their productivity. And because most theories of leadership are based on notions of political, organizational, or social power, they don't work too well with geeks.

If you want, or need, to lead geeks, you've got to jettison lots of what you already think about leadership and start over. This book will introduce you to the world of geek leadership and answer these and other questions:

- Who are geeks?
- What role do they play in today's businesses?
- How do geeks add value?
- How is their work structured and delivered?
- How can they be led and managed?
- How can they be integrated into the wider business organization?
- How can you improve the productivity of technology and technology workers?
- What can you do to motivate them?
- How are they different from other employees?
- Why are they so difficult to manage?

Although my primary experience is in the information technology arena, I focus here on issues common to all geekwork. Many of the principles and ideas discussed are equally applicable to scientific arenas such as biotech or pure research institutions. Many also apply to other forms of knowledge-intensive work, such as advertising, consulting, law, and architecture.

Who Will Benefit from This Book

This book is intended as a how-to guide for those who lead, manage, oversee, invest, or participate in technology projects. This is not a book about how to program a computer, install hardware, integrate software, select databases, design user interfaces, or even manage projects. This is a book about how to lead the *people*, the geeks, who do these essential things in your organization.

For executives who have become increasingly dependent on technology and the geeks who deliver technology for their success, this book will introduce you to the world of geeks, giving you the basic tools that you will need to integrate both technology and geeks into your organization.

For managers of nontechnological groups, this book will help you better understand and forge productive partnerships with geeks in all parts of the organization. Whether or not you are directly responsible for their day-to-day supervision, you need their help to get your job done.

For executives and managers within technological organizations, this book will help clarify your role as a manager and leader of these unique and critical people. It will help you move past simply managing technology and tasks and on to leading people. It will also help you to better align your organization with your client's needs and the organization's opportunities to leverage technology.

For project managers or aspiring project managers, this book provides foundational information that you'll need to deliver technology projects. Most project managers overemphasize the use of task lists, Gantt charts, budgets, and schedules as the means to successful project delivery, but these are just tools. Ultimately, all projects succeed or fail based on the work of people—the work of geeks who must be led, not just managed.

For human resource professionals, this book will help with the selection, hiring, counseling, and career development of technical people and organizations.

And for venture capitalists and board members of technical enterprises, this book will help you assess the leadership approach and potential of the companies that you either oversee or choose to invest in.

What's in This Book

The book is organized into four parts, each focusing on one facet of geek leadership.

In the Overview, "The Challenge of Geeks," Chapter One explores the roles of geeks and leaders within organizations.

Part One, "The Context of Geek Leadership," surveys several facets of the relationship among geeks, geekwork, leaders, and the organizations in which they live. The part introduction sets out the first of two primary models around which the book is structured: the Context of Geek Leadership model. Chapters Two and Three explore the distinctive culture of geeks, identifying patterns in the beliefs and behavior of individual geeks and the effects on geeks of working in groups. Chapter Four describes the uniqueness of the intricate, technical knowledge work performed by geeks and its effects on the relationship between geeks and leaders. And Chapter Five offers a model describing the twelve ways that knowledge workers deliver value to the organization. If you want to lead geeks, this will help you understand where to lead them.

Part Two covers the role and responsibilities of the geek leader. The part introduction sets out the second of the major models around which the book is structured: the Content of Geek Leadership model. Chapter Six discusses geek motivation and what leaders can do about it. Chapter Seven describes how geek leaders operate within their groups. Chapter Eight explores the geek leader's role in representing geeks to the world outside the cubicle. Chapter Nine introduces the subject of managing ambiguity and the hierarchy of ambiguity that must be resolved to lead successfully. It also discusses managing environmental ambiguity by exploring the broad, general questions that must be considered when helping to make sense of the environment in which geeks and leaders work. Chapter Ten sets out the questions that must be considered when structuring groups of geeks within an organization. And Chapter Eleven describes the geek leader's role in helping individuals be productive.

Chapter Twelve in the Conclusion discusses the tools that geek leaders use to transform the chaos of the creative workplace into a coherent and compelling place for geeks. The References section offers other resources for learning about the topics covered in the book. And finally, the Appendix collects in a single convenient place the checklists and models referenced throughout the book.

Marina del Rey, California   PAUL GLEN
September 2002

For Ethel Elcrat
(1899–1997)

Acknowledgments

No book is an island. Each one results from a collaboration of many people who deserve appreciation, and there are many whom I would like to thank for their contributions.

First, I thank Warren Bennis, without whom this book might never have been written or published. Long before I had the privilege of knowing him, his writing both informed and inspired me. I could not be more grateful for his invitation or honored by the inclusion of this book in his series. It speaks to his generosity that a world-famous author, professor, consultant, and speaker with endless demands on his time would voluntarily reach out to encourage and support the work of a younger and less established colleague.

I also express my appreciation to all of my clients who have invited me into their organizations and participated in the explorations of many of the ideas that appear in this book. Their drive to improve and to apply technology for the betterment of their organizations, employees, and customers challenges and inspires me.

Someone once told me that books were written one word at a time, but that's not entirely true. In fact, each word is written repeatedly, and many of them are appropriately left by the side of the road. Ron Rosman and Hillary Rettig were tirelessly supportive in the various stages of writing, offering ideas, challenging others, and smoothing presentation. They both showed incredible patience with incoherent early drafts. Their contributions have been immense, and I am truly grateful to both of them for their generous assistance.

Many others have also been exceptionally generous with their time, thoughts, and support. I appreciate the contributions of Alan Weiss, David Maister, David Finegold, Mary Lynn Reed, Linda Marsa, Rick Freedman, Dagmar Kamenar, Jan Hill, Vicki Millidge, Jeanette Polaschek, Jerald Savin, Marsha Lewin, Andrew Sobel, and Marian Cook.

I also express my thanks to those whose ideas I know only through their writings but have been essential to the shaping of this book. I am deeply indebted to Howard Gardner, Teresa Amabile, James MacGregor Burns, Steve McConnell, Ed Yourdon, Gerald Weinberg, Edgar Schein, Jim McCarthy, Henry Mintzberg, Watts Humphery, and Mihalyi Csikszentmihalyi.

I owe a lifetime of appreciation to my friends and mentors at SEI Information Technology, who have taught me so much over the years, including Fidelis Umeh, Pam Wiedenbeck, Yung Tsau, Greg Lewis, Kathy Radner, Lori Lunde, and Lonna Braverman.

Andrea Pedolsky was most helpful in guiding me through the intricacies of publishing law.

I thank the entire team at Jossey-Bass, including Susan Williams, Rob Brandt, Todd Berman, Jeff Wyneken, and Jesica Church. Every author should be so lucky to work with such a capable, professional, and helpful team.

I am deeply grateful to Beth Lazazzera, who has been unendingly patient with me throughout this project and has given her steadfast confidence and support.

And, of course, I thank my family: Ann, Marven, K, Cathy, Mitch, Ben, Elise, Isabel, Dorothy, and Bill.

P.G.

Leading Geeks

OVERVIEW

The Challenge of Geeks

1

Geeks, Leadership, and Geek Leadership

I hope that you have begun this book with a head full of questions:

- What's different about leading geeks from leading anyone else?
- What can I do to better leverage my organization's investment in these expensive, valuable, and temperamental employees?
- What makes geeks so difficult to manage?

You might even have some skeptical thoughts like these:

- What can this book teach me about leading geeks?
- Leadership is leadership, isn't it?

I welcome such questions—not because I think that I have every answer, but because that means you've already begun to consider how you interact with geeks or how you could. You're on your way to thinking about how the ideas and concepts in this book apply to you and your organization and how they might apply in the future.

This chapter lays the foundation by addressing some of these fundamental questions and explaining important concepts: who geeks are, why leading them is important, and how leadership of geeks differs from other types of leadership.

Geeks

Let's start out with geeks. The first thing to think about is who they are and why they are so important to your enterprise.

Who Are Geeks?

Geeks are the knowledge workers who specialize in the creation, maintenance, or support of high technology. They have job titles like programmer, product manager, project manager, quality assurance engineer, system designer, system architect, program manager, technical writer, help desk technician, deployment specialist, trainer, network manager, Web designer, database administrator, desktop support technician, or telecommunications specialist. Some of them may carry titles like chief information officer (CIO), chief knowledge officer (CKO), chief technical officer (CTO), development director, operations manager, and, on rare occasions, chief executive officer (CEO).

Thirty years ago, most geeks who found their way into the business world were part of the accounting department and were kept out of sight in the basement, tending to a single massive computer secured behind locked doors in an air-conditioned room. They were rarely seen outside their isolated environment and were known only by the people who read the piles of reports generated on wide green-lined paper.

Today they are everywhere. They may still be clustered in one large department or scattered as members of functional departments like accounting, marketing, product development, or manufacturing. Everyone knows who they are. They are the people you go to when your desktop computer or laptop stops working. The people you call when you think you might have a virus infecting your system. They're the people you consult when you dream up a new way of helping your clients by putting previously unavailable information on a Web site. You call them when you realize that you could save labor and costs by adding only one field to a screen of a current application.

If your company's product is high tech, you'll find them in product development, research, engineering, distribution, manufacturing, and support. Whether or not you sell a high-tech product or service, you will usually find them in the information technology (IT) department and probably working with accounting, finance, marketing, sales, and customer service.

In short, geeks are the highly intelligent, usually introverted, extremely valuable, independent-minded, hard-to-find, difficult-to-keep technology workers who are essential to the future of your company.

Why Geeks Matter

Despite all the hype and hurry surrounding the new economy, a few simple truths shine through the fog:

- Over the past three decades, the pace of technological change has increased.
- Technological innovation remains one of the most important components of an organization's ability to compete in the marketplace.
- Geeks are the people who deliver technological innovation.

Since the invention of the computer during World War II, information technology has been slowly penetrating organizations and transforming products, production methods, organizational structures, product flows, interorganizational relationships, customer relationships, and strategies. As computers have decreased in price and increased in power dramatically over this period, ever more creative applications have been built to reduce cost, improve service, develop new products, analyze data, and provide organizational infrastructure for communication.

And as information technology has enabled so many innovations, companies have become dependent on the people who create, maintain, and support these computers. It's the geeks who make it all go. Geeks have become among the most important human resources within almost every organization. As the technology they supply and support has become indispensable to almost every function of a company, geeks themselves have become indispensable too.

As they have moved further into organizations' functional areas, more and more managers come into contact with these unique and valuable employees. But they remain a mystery to most managers. Not only do they control strange, intricate, fragile, expensive, and indispensable systems, but as individuals they often prove hard to fathom. Corporate leaders, department managers, and functional managers who are perfectly capable of leading and managing in their area of specialty find geeks difficult to work with. Yet every leader, every sales manager, manufacturing manager, marketing specialist, accounting manager, customer service manager, purchasing manager, logistics manager, and human resource specialist must now be able to lead geeks. As each functional specialty within an organization becomes increasingly reliant on technology for its success, each person within those functional areas becomes reliant on his or her ability to interact with and lead geeks.

The Innovation Imperative

Whether or not you realize it, at this very moment, your organization is battling for its existence. No matter how profitable it has been, no matter how fast it has grown, no matter how loyal your employees, adoring your customers, or stratospheric your stock price, its future is in doubt. Whether you are in a nonprofit, a government agency, a small privately held business, or a publicly traded behemoth, your future is not assured.

All human institutions must constantly struggle to establish their relevance, attract attention, and mobilize resources to compete for survival. In the for-profit world, businesses compete in the marketplace for customers on the basis of value and price. If their value proposition proves insufficient or their price is beat out by competition, the organization must change, or ultimately it will fold. Similarly, if a nonprofit organization fails to offer sufficient value, it will ultimately fail to attract the resources of donors or the attention of the needy, and will collapse.

In this constant competition, no organization can afford to become static. It may change and evolve at different rates, but ultimately, to stagnate is to invite competition or lose relevance. If the needs and demands of the market shift and an organization fails to follow, it will be marginalized. If competition moves in to fulfill the same needs of the same population with a more compelling offering, the original group must adjust to the new reality or risk losing relevance.

Successful organizations—ones that persist and maintain their relevance over long periods of time—meet that challenge with innovation. They continually strive to refine their value proposition. Occasionally, they may reinvent themselves completely, revisiting and redefining their overarching purpose, but usually innovation happens on a much smaller scale. They incrementally improve their products and services, raising value, lowering cost, or expanding markets. In this way, they constantly align with demands and meet competitive pressures.

Geeks and Innovation

So if organizations constantly need to renew their relevance, where do they turn for innovation? It would be tempting to answer "geeks," but that wouldn't be entirely true. The types of creativity and insight needed to reinvigorate an organization with innovative products, services, and processes can come from almost anywhere. But regardless of where ideas come from, increasingly you need geeks to implement them.

Ideas for new or enhanced products or services come from many places: customers, marketing, sales, manufacturing, product development, and product support. If the product is high tech, you need geeks to analyze the feasibility and design of new or enhanced products. But even if your product is more conventional, most new ideas include some information content within either the physical product or the production or distribution. Again, you need geeks.

Service and process innovations have become similarly information intensive and require geeks for implementation. Most innovations in services today are enabled by information technology. The interconnection of massive databases combined with the access to the Web has opened many new ways to service customers' information and transaction needs. Banking customers now expect to view all of their accounts in one place, at one time, with the click of a mouse in a Web browser or through personal financial management software like Quicken or Microsoft Money.

Geeks can also be a valuable source of ideas for innovation. Given their intimate knowledge of products and processes, they often find better ways to do things. They can be an integral part of the creative process of envisioning new products and services, as well as the processes and procedures to produce them.

To sum up, geeks are essential to innovation, and innovation is essential to the future of all enterprises. Without geeks in your enterprise, your future is in doubt.

Simply having geeks is not enough. They must be effectively integrated into the organization and focused on appropriate tasks. In other words, the future of your organization depends, along with other things, on your ability to lead geeks effectively.

Leadership

Organizations need leadership for more than just making the best use of technology and geeks. They need leadership to remain vibrant, living, relevant institutions that serve the needs of their stakeholders. Businesses need leaders to energize their staffs and focus their attention.

Yet despite the near universal longing for leaders, leadership itself remains elusive. Scholars have been studying great leaders as individuals and leadership as a subject for centuries. Yet there's surprisingly little consensus among the various views about what actu-ally constitutes leadership.

Popular conceptions of leadership represent a unidirectional relationship between one leader and many followers. Leaders not only direct followers to do specific things; they have the power to enforce their wishes. Whether the source of that power is extraor-dinary ability, coercive authoritarian force, charisma, moral virtue, or organizational legitimacy, leaders are in a position to dictate the actions of their followers unilaterally.

In fact, the ideas of leadership and power have become so inti-mately intertwined that they are often used interchangeably. It's not uncommon to hear that the prime minister of a country is referred to as the leader of a country or of a CEO of a corporation being referred to as a leader of the company. But it's equally clear that many people who hold these positions do not necessarily provide leadership. The president of a company may be only its chief bureaucrat or head salesperson and not necessarily its leader. The prime minister of a country may be only the head administrator of the government and not the leader of the people. It's also clear that although the president or prime minister may not provide leader-ship, these are still powerful people. They have a great deal of abil-ity to impose their will on others. To explore the relationship between leadership and power in more detail, read James MacGre-gor Burns's classic Pulitzer Prize–winning book *Leadership*.

Although we often speak of power as if it were a physical object like a ham sandwich, it's not. One cannot actually hold power, cling to it, or relinquish it. You may be able to treat a symbol of power as an object, such as a crown, scepter, rank insignia, or vestment. But that's not the same as the actual power. Those are just physical objects meant to represent power.

Power is one facet of the complex relationships between human beings. A person is said to be powerful based on the degree to which he or she can exert control over the actions of one or more other people through any available means. The exercise of power may take many forms, ranging from inspiration to intimidation, from bribery to promises, from seduction to torture. A powerful person can effect the behavior of a less powerful person despite any objections from the less powerful person.

But is the exercise of raw power the same as leadership? Clearly not. Although leaders are powerful, not all powerful people are leaders. There are many brutal dictators who clearly have substantial power, yet few would call them leaders.

The holders of power need not be concerned with the interests of those over whom they hold power. They may affect others' behaviors to satisfy their own wishes, or further their own selfish ends, or benefit the condition of the less powerful.

Leadership is not so one-sided a relationship. Leaders exercise their power to further the commonly held goals of both the leaders and the followers. In this way, leadership is a special type of power relationship in which both leaders and followers are mutually influential for their mutual benefit.

Although many scholars and writers have gone to great lengths to tease apart the concepts of management and leadership, I will not make that distinction in this book. Although I accept that there are differences between the two, separating them out does not offer significant value for this discussion. We are examining leadership in one limited domain, where the distinction is relatively unimportant. Were we looking at political leadership of a country, the difference might be much more instructive.

In the world of geek leadership, one person usually supplies both management and leadership simultaneously and must be able to handle the demands of both. In the course of one meeting, or even in the course of one minute, a manager may have to pay attention to both a leader's grand strategy and a minute tactic.

More important than noting the distinctions between leadership and management is recognizing their commonality and confluence in the technical environment. Both are focused on providing guidance to the *people* who deliver technology rather than the tasks or the technology itself. Too often, managers work under the misapprehension that their job is to manage a project or a task list rather than the people who perform the tasks.

Why Geek Leadership Is Different

Why do we need a special book devoted only to geeks when bookstore shelves are groaning under the weight of leadership books already? In part because many of those books make the point implicitly or explicitly that whom you are leading is essentially irrelevant and that effective leaders can lead anyone. But leading geeks is, in fact, different from leading others. There are three distinct reasons to look at geek leadership differently from more traditional approaches:

- Geeks are different from other people.
- Geekwork is different from other work.
- Power is useless with geeks.

Geeks Are Different

Geeks are different from other people. If this comes as a shocking statement to you, you're either oblivious to others or unusually charitable with your opinions about others. But let's face it: stereotypes exist for a reason, and although they can be cruel and insensitive, they often contain a kernel of truth. For geeks, it's certainly true.

Most writers on leadership, while acknowledging that leadership is a relationship between a leader and a group of followers, fail to acknowledge that the nature of the follower has anything to do with the nature of the relationship.

So the first thing you must recognize if you want to lead geeks is that geeks are different. Then you must accept *how* they're different from other employees. This is not about judging anybody, just recognizing their differences. And then you have to adjust your leadership style to be productive with geeks. I'm not suggesting that you need to be disingenuous or phony. In fact, if you were, you would immediately set off any geek's hypocrisy detector. Still, you do need to adjust as you would in any relationship to the nature of others.

Geekwork Is Different

Not only are geeks different from other employees, but their work is quite different as well. Although it may not be obvious at first, the nature of geekwork imprints itself on the relationship between a leader and geeks just as much as the personality of geeks and leaders does.

When examining relationships in general, and work relationships in particular, we often underestimate the influence that the nature of the work imparts to both the organizational culture and individual relationships. The structure of day-to-day tasks imposes its own patterns of thinking on those who engage with them on an ongoing basis, and the assumptions induced by the work permeate the relationship among manager, leader, and follower. All are affected by the influence of the work. And in this case, geekwork imparts its own unique behavioral and cognitive patterns on the leadership relationship.

Power Is Useless with Geeks

The final reason that leading geeks is different from leading others is the diminished role that power plays in the relationship between leader and followers. Traditionally, leadership is conceptualized as a special form of power relationship where leaders have substantial influence over the behavior of followers and exercises that power for mutual benefit.

But here geekwork intervenes in the relationship and undermines power as a useful basis for the relationship between leader and geeks. While a manager may have substantial authority and power to control the behavior of geeks, behavior plays a much smaller role in the successful completion of geekwork than in other forms of work. Geekwork is less about behavior and more about thought, ideas, and the application of creativity.

In more traditional forms of work, controlling employee behavior is the primary point of management. If the assembly worker responsible for attaching the wheel to the front of a car attaches that wheel to the car, then he has fulfilled his primary function: his behavior has delivered value. If a short-order cook at a restaurant accepts orders, cooks food, and hands it to the server, he has fulfilled his task. For geeks, it's different.

For geeks, behavior plays a much smaller part in the delivery of value. A programmer may sit at his desk all day and type keys on the keyboard quietly without bothering anyone else, but if he's typed a sonnet instead of a program, it's of no value to the organization.

With geekwork, you are attempting to harness the creativity of individuals and groups in its purest form. And although behavior plays a role, it is substantially less important than in almost any other form of work.

Because power is about the regulation of behavior, it has very little effect on creativity. Traditional methods of exercising control have little positive effect on the inner state of mind of geeks. And so power itself becomes substantially less important a facet of the relationship between leaders and geeks.

We must rethink what it means to lead in the face of geekwork because most conceptions of leadership are intimately tied to notions of power.

What Is Geek Leadership?

To account for the reduction in the role of power and acknowledge the uniqueness of geeks and geekwork, we need to take a step back and rebuild what it means to lead these unique employees. Two models help encapsulate what it takes to lead in this environment: the Context of Geek Leadership and the Content of Geek Leadership.

My goal here is not to discard the brilliant reasoning about power and leadership that has occurred over the past thousand years, but instead to adopt and adapt what we already know about leadership to this relatively new environment. As we explore the implications of these two models, you will find both familiar and unfamiliar ideas about leadership. Many elements of the common wisdom about leadership carry over unchanged, unaffected by the environment of technological innovation; others must be turned on their head and radically altered.

The Context of Geek Leadership

In order to function effectively as a leader in this environment it is necessary to first have a better picture of the lay of land. This model is designed to help establish both new and familiar roadmarks about the relationships of geeks, leaders, geekwork, organizational culture, and the broader sociopolitical environment (Figure 1.1).

A three-way relationship, which I call the tripartite relationship between geeks, leaders, and geekwork, lies at the center of this

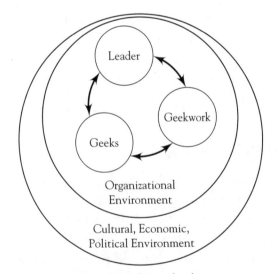

FIGURE 1.1. The Context of Geek Leadership.

model. Ordinarily, leadership relationships are discussed only as having two categories of parties: leaders and followers. But in the geek environment, the unique nature of geekwork, the highly abstract, creative, technical work imposes so many demands on both geeks and leaders that you can think of it as a third party to the relationship.

To help make sense of the technical environment, first we will examine geeks and geekwork in considerable detail. Geeks as individuals and in groups are quite different from most other people, bringing to the workplace their own culture, values, and needs, which must be accommodated.

The Content of Geek Leadership

The second model, the Content of Geek Leadership, describes the role, responsibilities, and tasks of the geek leader. Adjusting more traditional views of leadership to accommodate the unusual nature of the geek environment, this model describes the four key responsibilities of the geek leader. In contrast to the conventional model of hierarchical command and control, this leader plays a more enabling role, providing internal facilitation, furnishing external representation, nurturing motivation, and helping to manage ambiguity (Figure 1.2).

To contrast the Content of Geek Leadership with more conventional ideas about the responsibilities and tasks of leaders, let's take a look at an analogous simplifying model of traditional leadership (Figure 1.3). Some of the tasks and responsibilities change relatively little, but others are radically different.

Both traditional and geek leaders furnish external representation almost identically. And although both seek to motivate followers, their methods are remarkably different due to the nature of geeks and geekwork. Conventional leaders focus their attention on directing the activities of followers rather than providing internal facilitation, and they make decisions rather than actively managing ambiguity.

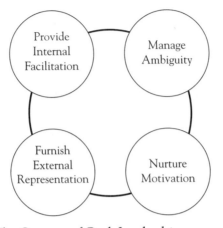

FIGURE 1.2. The Content of Geek Leadership.

Perhaps the most important difference is in traditional leaders' concentration on establishing and maintaining a power base. All of the responsibilities and tasks of conventional leadership are driven by a leader's ability to apply power to enforce decisions, direct activities, and motivate followers. For the geek leader, power is substantially less important for moving an organization.

Harmonizing Content and Context

Geeks are best able to function at peak efficiency when everything makes sense. When they understand the mission, vision, and values of their overall organization; can clearly articulate their role within the organization; recognize technology's part in fulfilling the organization's goals; and feel that the values of the organization are consistently upheld by leaders and followers alike, they are able to become highly motivated and remarkably productive. Complete harmony is a rare and fragile state, but when all of these stars align, political and emotional barriers to productivity fall.

A geek leader's goal is to build and maintain a state of harmonized content and context. Using the role and tasks of the geek leader, the leader creates and embodies a defining narrative that helps geeks make sense of all the disparate facts of their work world

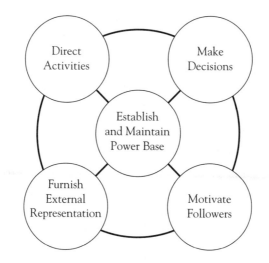

FIGURE 1.3. The Content of Traditional Leadership.

fulfilling the essential human needs of the people who deliver technology. When their human needs are fulfilled, they are free to focus on fulfilling an organization's technical needs.

Summary

FUNDAMENTAL QUESTIONS

- Why worry about geeks?
- What is leadership?
- Why is leading geeks different from leading other employees?
- What's in this book, and how will it help me learn to lead geeks?

KEY IDEAS

- Geeks, as the creators and keepers of technology, are essential to every organization's ability to innovate and remain vibrant and viable.

- Because technology has permeated all functional areas of organizations, every manager must now know how to lead geeks.

- Many traditional approaches to leadership don't work when it comes to leading geeks for three key reasons: geeks are different from other people, geekwork is different from other work, and power is useless with geeks.

- This book offers two simplifying models to help clarify geek leadership: the Context of Geek Leadership describes the environment in which geek leadership takes place, and the Content of Geek Leadership describes the tasks and responsibilities of a geek leader.

- The ultimate goal of geek leadership is to harmonize the content and context in order to drive the productivity and creativity of geeks.

PART ONE

The Context of Geek Leadership

Few successful business strategies are developed by managers without a clear understanding of the competition, product, and customers. If someone presented you with a strategic plan that ignored the context of your business, you probably wouldn't even bother reading it. So it is with leading geeks. If you don't understand and acknowledge the environment in which geeks live and work, you are unlikely to become an effective leader of geeks (see Figure 1.1 in Chapter One).

An old myth about leadership says that if you can lead in one environment, you can lead in any environment. Unfortunately, it's not true. All too often leaders, who are by nature people of action, are too eager to focus on their own tasks and activities without a thorough understanding of context. This is why so many managers fail when trying to lead high-tech work. It's very easy to make the mistake of assuming that what works in leading salespeople, marketers, or logistics people will automatically work in every environment, but the context of geekwork is very different. Much of what works with others may be ineffective or even counterproductive in the geek environment.

To help clarify this critical background information, Part One presents an overview of the first of the two central models of the book, the Context of Geek Leadership. It is intended to provide a simplifying framework for understanding the complex relationship

of leaders, geeks, and geekwork and the organizational, sociopolitical, and economic environment in which these relationships take
place.

Leaders

The role of the geek leader is one without a popular mythology.
Many leadership roles have commonly understood images that
shape our thinking about them. If I were to mention the name of a
Fortune 500 CEO, a dictator, or a university president, you would
probably conjure up an image that you associate with that type of
person. But if I were to mention the name of a CIO, you probably
wouldn't have any image to recall. The lack of mythology may contribute to the difficulty in assuming this role.

One of the most common questions about leading geeks is,
"Who makes a good geek leader, and what background do they typically come from?" The answer is that there is no one source for
geek leaders. They can come from a variety of backgrounds. They
may come from a technical background, emerging from their peers
as a natural leader by virtue of technical competence or personality.
But it's not required that they have strong technical skills. You can
lead geeks without these skills—but only if you have a healthy
respect for the limits of your own knowledge of the details of technical work. Geek leaders may be entrepreneurs who develop a
vision to serve a market with a product or service that is enabled by
technology. For these leaders, the passion for their client and their
product places them at the head of a group of geeks.

Geek leaders may be corporate technology managers such as
CIO, CTO, or CKO. Many of these managers rise through the
ranks of large technology organizations with well-defined job hierarchies, entrenched bureaucracies, and rigorous procedures. Others
in the same positions may have spent their careers in other functional business areas and lack a technological background altogether.

Geek leaders may be managers or executives from nontechnical areas of the business such as marketing, operations, or manufacturing. Because technology permeates every facet of business life, every manager must become a geek leader to some extent. But like it or not, just knowing your functional area and how to lead the people in it is no longer sufficient. Few can afford to plod along without the innovation that geeks help provide.

Ultimately, every geek leader has one primary goal: to capture, apply, and leverage the creative work of geeks to enable business operations, improve efficiency, develop competitive products, fulfill regulatory requirements, provide management information, speed production, or improve customer service.

The role of the geek leader is the subject of Part Two of this book, so will not be discussed in detail in this part.

Geeks

Geeks are the enablers of technology who develop, deploy, and support the systems and products that deliver value to customers and help companies remain competitive. They are the indispensable enablers of innovation.

But many leaders find the ways and work of geeks baffling. To some managers, walking into the IT department feels almost like walking into a foreign country where they don't speak the language and are baffled by the culture. For geeks, the business environment is similarly mysterious. They often struggle with understanding the culture of other groups, the needs of users, and the interests of managers and leaders. They find the values and behaviors of nontechnical people to be just as confusing as others find theirs. As a group, they are most resistant to leadership yet may be more in need of it than any other group of employees.

In general, geeks bring a cynical eye to their relationship with leaders. They don't accept leadership easily and are suspicious about the motives of those who would direct them. This cynicism often cripples leadership relationships from the start, placing them under strain before they have even been established.

To understand geeks, you must first understand their nature as individuals. You need to understand the patterns of values and assumptions that they bring to the workplace, the attitudes that they display, and the meanings of their behaviors. You must understand the group dynamics of geeks in the workplace. Since most geekwork is done in groups, it's important to understand the nature of the tribe.

And finally, you must understand the nature of the relationship between geeks and their geekwork. Long before they engage with you as a leader, they engage with geekwork. There's a powerful bond between a geek and his technology that transcends any particular project or company or leader.

The nature of geeks is discussed at length in Chapters Two and Three. Chapter Two, "The Essential Geek," takes a look at the patterns of attitudes, assumptions, and values of geeks as individuals. This chapter is intended to provide you with a basic appreciation of the perspective of geeks. Chapter Three, "Groups of Geeks," explores the dynamics of geeks in groups.

Geekwork

Geekwork encompasses a wide variety of activities and the production of different artifacts—for example:

- Technological product such as software or hardware
- The process of creating the design for technological products
- The artifacts of the process of creating the design for technological products, such as documentation, project plans, risk assessments, budgets, staffing plans, testing plans, technology assessment, and status reports
- The identification of options for applying technology to business
- Directed research and development

- Experimentation and development of new processes
- Recruiting geeks

By its very nature, geekwork is highly ambiguous and requires the application of creativity, technological knowledge, business acumen, and collaborative skills. Because of its ambiguity and emphasis on thought over action, it demands an unusual style of work that is more akin to professional service than to traditional corporate work.

The relentless ambiguity of geekwork imprints itself on both geeks and leaders, as well as the relationship between them. This is why, in this model, I have elevated geekwork to equal partnership in what would ordinarily be a two-way relationship between leaders and followers.

Chapters Four and Five examine the role geekwork plays in the relationship between leaders and geeks in more detail. Chapter Four, "The Nature of Geekwork," explores how geekwork differs from more ordinary work and how that affects both geeks and leaders. Chapter Five, "Performing Geekwork," describes in detail the skills and abilities necessary for geeks to succeed within technological organizations.

The Tripartite Relationship

Geeks, leaders, and geekwork are inseparable from one another within an organizational context. Together, they form a constellation, each enabling the other but at the same time also imposing constraints. Without geeks, leaders would have no followers to implement and support technology. Without leaders, geeks would lack direction. And without geekwork, neither would be effective at implementing change.

Ordinarily, in the work environment, leadership can be considered a two-way relationship between leaders and followers and analyzed without significant interference from the work at hand. But because geekwork is so unusual, it imposes its own demands on geeks and leaders affecting the relationship. The constraints of geekwork are so unusual that it becomes nearly impossible to understand the relationship between geeks and leaders without understanding the mediation of geekwork.

All three members of the tripartite relationship are ultimately focused on organizational change. Leaders devote most of their energy to envisioning, planning, and implementing changes within an organization to renew its relevance or develop its competitiveness. The technology resulting from geekwork is usually intended to enable change. And geeks devote their energies to enabling technology.

As they work together to implement organizational change, geeks, leaders, and geekwork all impose constraints on the others over time. Technological limitations affect both leaders and geeks, often preventing them from completely realizing their visions. The nature of geekwork both empowers leaders and geeks at the same time as it constrains them.

In addition to the constraints that geekwork imposes on geeks and leaders, the relationship is affected by a clash of cultures. Joseph Raelin describes this dynamic in his book *Clash of Cultures: Managers Managing Professionals*. Although the tripartite relationship exists in a single organizational culture, managers and geeks each bring the cultural assumptions of their respective disciplines. The managerial subculture with its emphasis on power, politics, tasks, and progress rarely integrates easily with geek subculture with its focus on creativity, fun, openness, independence, and competition.

The Organizational Environment

The interlocking tripartite relationship among geeks, leaders, and geekwork does not take place in a vacuum. All three live within an immediate organizational context that directly affects all aspects of the relationship. The organizational context includes fundamental assumptions about the following factors:

- Organizational goals and purpose
- Products
- Markets
- Customers
- Marketing channels
- Competition
- Processes
- Organizational structures
- Hierarchy
- Power
- Priorities

In some organizations, these are explicitly discussed and apparent in the day-to-day life. For others, these may be deeply held but unarticulated beliefs that drive behavior in subtle ways. But for most organizations, these assumptions emerge from experience and are unarticulated and elusive. In addition, organizations generally do not have a monolithic culture; rather, they are conglomerations of many subcultures and subgroups. Different subgroups have their own ideas and agendas that conflict with one another and change over time.

On these shifting sands, the tripartite relationship is built, and as they shift, so too must the relationship. For example, as organizational priorities shift, the selection of geekwork will change. If a company realizes that it must offer a new high-tech product to remain competitive in its market, then projects will be immediately organized to design and deliver the product.

Other effects are more subtle but no less influential. For example, managers of functional areas are recruited by executives in the wider organization, who generally select peers who conform to their own conception of what leaders should be like. Many studies have shown that given a choice, managers usually prefer to hire people similar to themselves. Through selection of leaders, the tripartite relationship will be strongly affected by outside managers' previously developed ideas about hierarchy, control, openness, and work style.

Once the tripartite relationship has been established, it can also be difficult to integrate it into the broader organizational environment. As leaders and geeks concur about how they will interact with each other, they may find that their assumptions conflict with those of the broader organization and are challenged, or even undermined, by others. Cultural norms selected by geeks and leaders may fly in the face of entrenched attitudes toward power, hierarchy, autonomy, openness, goals, process, and office decorum.

In this environment, it is often hard to align the goals and purposes of geeks and geek leaders with those of the organization. Difficulties can stem from diverging priorities, but more often they result from inadequately articulated or constantly changing ideas about direction.

The Sociopolitical and Economic Environment

Finally, the entire organization exists in the context of the broader society. Organizations are constantly buffeted by changes in the local, national, and international economy; the competitive landscape; the regulatory environment; the international political climate; availability of capital; and demographic, technological, and social trends.

2

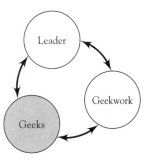

The Essential Geek

"How do you know that a geek is an extrovert?"
"He's looking at *your* shoes."

Stereotypes about geeks abound. Unfashionably dressed, pimply, video-game-playing young boys rolling Dungeons and Dragons dice populate the comic pages of most major daily newspapers. Rich, self-absorbed, intelligent, ruthless entrepreneurs line the Market-place Section of the *Wall Street Journal*. Kindly, wise, absent-minded professors dream brilliant yet unintelligible thoughts in their ivory towers and yet can't remember how to tie their shoes.

Whether you consider such images funny, crude, or cruel, they are not particularly useful for you, the real-life leader seeking to drive a geek-powered organization. These vague images provide you with little information that will help you direct, monitor, control, or motivate individuals or groups. In fact, they may misdirect you into counterproductive directions.

In this chapter, we examine geeks, the first member of the tripartite relationship.[1] We will move past useless stereotypes and look into the patterns of geek attitudes, beliefs, and behaviors that make them both unusual and unusually difficult to understand and lead. This list is not based on some abstract psychological theory, but on more than fifteen years working with, leading, managing, coaching, and cajoling geeks in academic and business environments. The goal is to illuminate and provide a foundation for later discussions, not to provide guidance about how to deal with the phenomena described. All we are trying to do here is to understand geeks as individuals better.

Obviously, not every geek you meet will conform to all the patterns described. Individuals are just that: individual. Nevertheless, that doesn't mean that we can't make some useful generalizations to help guide us in making these groups more effective. One generalization that I won't make relates to gender. Geekdom knows no gender boundaries. Although it is true that there are more male than female geeks, it's not particularly important in understanding them. The patterns of attitudes, beliefs, and behaviors stem from the common assumptions of those who are drawn to technical work.

Passion for Reason

According to Rick Freedman, author of *The IT Consultant*, "The connection between Star Trek and geeks is not accidental. It's also not surprising that Mr. Spock is such a popular character."[2] Mr. Spock's cool, emotionless detachment holds an almost mystical appeal for geeks. More than thirty years after the television show was canceled, you can still buy photographs of Mr. Spock to take home and hang over your candles to create a small altar to his near-divinity. His self-control, relentless logic, and commitment to rationality offer a model to which all geekdom aspires.

Geeks revere the rational. The irony is that their boundless faith in reason is fired by passion, a conviction so strong that it can only be based in emotion—the inherently irrational. The emotional force behind their reason is staggering. Cross it at your own peril.

Reason is a comfortable place for geeks, providing a certainty and a grounding that emotion lacks. Passions come and go, and they are unpredictable and ferocious. For a geek, to reason is to know, and to know is to be certain, and to be certain is to be right, and to be right is to be safe.

This need for safety, for security, for the calming shelter of reason runs deep. It runs through time, back to the philosophers and mathematicians on whose work science and technology are built.

You can feel this passion for reason in the ideas of philosophers like Descartes, Leibniz, Spinoza, Fermat, and Pascal. Especially for those like Descartes, whose desire to systematize knowledge and raise human reason to an equal position with faith, the creativity, force of will, and bravery in challenging the dogma of the day could only have been fired by a passion for reason.

Again ironically, today's geeks may look to reason more fervently than did their predecessors. Even Pascal did not attempt to forge reason and emotion so closely. Faith still occupied an *equal* position to reason, not a superior one. In his unfinished book *Pensées*, a defense of the Catholic religion, Pascal observed, "The heart has its reasons, which reason does not know."

The views of many of today's geeks are not so forgiving. Many believe that *all* things must have reasons and that *all* decisions must be reasonable. To attempt to pass faulty logic or vague feelings as reasons for decisions with which they disagree is to invite conflict. The passion of truth can transform the most timid of geeks into a fierce opponent.

Problem-Solution Mind-Set

Every discipline favors certain mental tools over others. Economists use mathematical models. Scientists use hypothesis and experiments. Musicians use scales, notes, and measures. Technical geeks use problems and solutions.

It's easy to overlook how the structure of daily work colors how we see the world. We learn to be successful in our chosen fields by applying the mental tools of the trade. We learn which ways of thinking work and which don't through experimentation with the application of various approaches. Those that work well are retained; those that don't are discarded. Through repetition, those that work begin to organize how we approach almost anything that's thrown our way.

For geeks, the mental tool that organizes almost every situation is the problem-solution model. When confronted with almost any situation, the initial response is to seek out *the* problem and then find *the* solution. It doesn't matter that many situations don't conform to this model. For example, geeks almost universally despise status meetings, which they consider, at best, a waste of time, and often micromanagement, one of the greatest offenses a manager can offer. For geeks, meetings don't conform to the problem-solution model of work. A meeting can't be clearly identified as solving a particular problem, so it must be a waste.

Early Success

There's a persistent image of geeks as young prodigies, and it's not entirely without merit. Especially for those in the computer field, it's not uncommon for their talents to become apparent early in life. They tend to be drawn to computers at an early age. Not that I was a prodigy, but I bought my first computer (with an amazing 4K of memory) with my paper route money while I was still in elementary school.

The computer whiz kid is the one all the teachers go to (or point at) when the systems in the school lab or audiovisual equipment are broken. Technology-challenged parents turn to tech-savvy kids to help decode the mysteries of the household PC, DVD, and other systems. They become service providers to the adults in their lives.

When these talents are revealed, whiz kids become a resource for friends, teachers, parents, siblings, and neighbors. They become the center of attention and appreciation. And these early experiences have notable lasting effects.

People learn through experience. They are faced with situations, respond to them, and receive feedback, positive and negative. For strong learners, negative feedback results in trying something different the next time a similar situation is faced. Positive feedback usually results in repeating the same behaviors. Just like rats in a maze, if there's cheese at the same place every time, why go anywhere else?

With young prodigies, this sort of dynamic often comes into play. They are rewarded early in life for their aptitudes and demonstrations. Not only does that leave them with positive reinforcement for their technical successes, it rewards them for their behaviors as well. People tend to grow and mature more from pain than from comfort, but many young geeks are treated to early success. Often they are not forced to develop the social skills that many others are.

Many geeks as a result retain a somewhat childlike outlook on the world, for better and worse. It shows itself in their curiosity and playfulness. But it can also show in insensitivity, lack of self-awareness, and condescension.

Joy of Puzzles

Geeks love intellectual activities. The engagement of knowledge, creativity, and logic is a lifelong pursuit for them. In many ways, that activity is distilled into its essence in the form of puzzles.

A puzzle can take many forms. It can be something from the morning newspaper like a crossword or a word search. It can be a riddle or a word game like an anagram. It can be formulated as a mathematical query or even the dreaded word problem. It can also be delivered in the form of a statement, such as a specification for a piece of software.

Each of these is a call not to action but to thought. Each challenge tests one's ability to answer that call. To a geek, a puzzle is an opportunity to exercise the mind, prove competence, or foil the puzzle master who formulated the question. It doesn't matter if that challenge is a simple math problem or President Kennedy's call to put a man on the moon.

Most people are uninterested by such challenges. These problems either have no practical result or are too difficult to bother with. Geeks, to the contrary, revel in them. There is little else more engaging to a geek than a difficult, clever, and witty brainteaser. It is in the concentration to defeat these riddles that they find complete engagement—the experience that Mihaly Csikszentmihalyi, a psychologist and professor at the Peter F. Drucker Graduate

School of Management, part of Claremont Graduate University, calls flow. Flow is the experience in which high task skill and challenge meet and result in an experience of effortless productivity and engagement—"being in the zone," he calls it. According to Csikszentmihalyi, "It is in the full involvement of flow, rather than happiness, that makes for excellence in life":

> When goals are clear, feedback relevant, and challenges and skills are in balance, attention becomes ordered and fully invested. Because of the total demand on psychic energy, a person in flow is completely focused. There is no space in consciousness for distracting thoughts, irrelevant feelings. Self-consciousness disappears, yet one feels stronger than usual. The sense of time is distorted: hours seem to pass by in minutes. When a person's entire being is stretched in the full functioning of body and mind, whatever one does becomes worth doing for its own sake; living becomes its own justification. In the harmonious focusing of physical and psychic energy, life finally comes into its own.[3]

Geeks seek this peak experience in their puzzles.

Curiosity

Reality is endlessly fascinating to geeks. It is perhaps the ultimate puzzle.

Geeks tend to be rich in natural curiosity. Their curiosity does not always extend in the same directions as that of non-geeks. They generally don't have an insatiable desire to know what's going on in the love life of their favorite celebrity. They rarely want to keep up with soap operas. They're really not interested in the latest fashion trends.

They are, however, always trying to figure out how something works. As children, they take apart their toys to see what's inside. The better ones even put the toys back together. The ambitious ones try to improve the toy's function. Whether examining a cosmological theory, a car, or a computer, geeks have no choice but to examine its inner workings.

Their curiosity tends to remain unaltered throughout life, although the subject of their examinations may shift over time. Some geeks stay focused on a single avenue of exploration through-out life, while others change focus on a regular basis. Regardless, this insatiable desire to know the workings of machines, software, or ideas drives many geek activities.

In addition to the shifting of the subjects of inquiries, geeks differ from one another in the types of phenomena that they examine. Some are abstract thinkers and want to understand concepts and principles. Others are more mechanical and need to touch and feel their subject.

One important point to note as a leader of geeks is that curiosity, so essential to performing geekwork, sometimes can run amok. Geeks can become so engrossed in some technical task that they begin to explore it far beyond what's necessary to complete the job. For example, I sometimes spend way too much time tweaking the configuration of my computers just for the joy of seeing how fast I can make them go. I know that whatever time I save by having a faster computer will be far outweighed by the time I wasted exploring, but the curiosity can be hard to ignore.

Geeks Choose Machines

It's 2:00 A.M. The only sound in the darkened room is the rapid, rhythmic click of a computer keyboard. Were it not for the bluish glow of the monitor, it would be impossible to see the desk cluttered with scraps of paper, piles of open manuals, and half-eaten food. The occupant, dressed only in a T-shirt and shorts, doesn't know what time it is, and he doesn't care. He is engrossed, completely submerged. And it's his day off.

The image of the lonely nerd is now firmly established in our culture. And although it's not true for all geeks, it does carry a kernel of truth. Whereas few business executives would run home to analyze a balance sheet, many geeks do race home to their systems, manuals, and technical journals. It's not uncommon to find true geeks immersed in their technology as much during their off-hours as during work.

Don't confuse this with being consumed by their work. It's the toys that consume them, not the work. Work is the means to the end. The passion is not so much what technology can do, but the joy in understanding how it works.

The key point here is not that geeks love technology, but that given a choice between spending time with technology or with people, they generally choose technology. For most, this is a preference that begins early in life and can continue indefinitely. As geeks age, partner, and have families, the all-consuming passion for technology sometimes fades, but the imprint of the early years is always there. When they are stressed or confused, it will reappear. Geeks are generally introverts.

Self-Expression = Communication

I recently witnessed a consultant and her geeky client having a serious argument. The consultant had created a custom class for the client's staff. She had prepared customized materials, shipped books, traveled to the city, rented a classroom, hired me to coteach, and set up for the class. We arrived at 8:00 A.M. to set up the room for a 9:00 A.M. class. We loaded up the computer with slides, rearranged the furniture, laid out the student books, hung posters on the walls, and checked with the caterers. Everything was ready. The entire student experience was prepared perfectly.

Nine o'clock came and went, and none of the students showed up. Around 10:00 A.M., she was finally able to reach the client by telephone. The conversation that ensued was, to say the least, a bit heated. Passions were inflamed. Voices were raised. It turned out that he told his people that the class started at 1:00 P.M., not 9:00 A.M. Clearly, there had been a miscommunication, but he steadfastly refused to accept any responsibility. He just kept repeating, "I was clear about that." The consultant was clear that she was willing to accept her part in the miscommunication, but wanted to engage the client in a conversation about how to fix the problem. He couldn't accept any responsibility, and he couldn't get past the blame discussion to try to fix the problem.

The client had fallen into the classic trap of believing that saying something is the same thing as communicating it. Who was right or wrong in the argument doesn't matter. The result of the miscommunication was no different regardless of who misunderstood whom. It also doesn't matter because it takes two people to fail to communicate. Whether or not he had actually expressed his desire for the class to begin in the afternoon, his protest was more telling than he realized. Whether or not he had been clear, his message had not been communicated.

Effective communication occurs when a thought of one person is translated into words, expressed, heard, and translated back into an identical thought in the mind of another. In 1928, English literary critic and author I. A. Richards wrote, "Communication takes place when one mind so acts upon its environment that another mind is influenced, and in that other mind an experience occurs which is like the experience in the first mind, and is caused in part by that experience."[4]

Whether or not the client had translated his thought about the starting time into words and expressed it or not, the message had not been received. He felt that his job in communication ended with self-expression. Reception is someone else's problem. Geeks don't have an exclusive right to this misconception, but it's particularly embedded in geek culture.

My Facts Are Your Facts

Although geeks generally are clear, careful thinkers, they can get very sloppy about the differences among facts, assumptions, opinions, inferences, and implications. This often results in unnecessary embarrassment or conflict.

Almost every manager of geeks has a story something like this one, which Rick Freedman told me. At the time, Rick was the regional manager for the Kansas City office of a national technology consultancy and was visiting a potential client. He had brought along a technical consultant to provide additional information at the sales meeting. The meeting was set up for the CIO of the company and several of his direct reports, including the organization's CTO, who had just led the installation of the new network system.

The technical consultant had spent about a day looking at the client's systems to provide an initial impression of the work that would be required. At some point in the meeting, the CTO turned to the consultant and asked what he thought of the new system. The consultant responded, "Well, you've got Windows NT 3.51 installed on a number of your systems. Only an idiot would put that in." The room fell silent. Not only had he just insulted the systems of the client, he had personally insulted the CTO, who was sitting in the room. Obviously, they didn't get the job.

Oddly, the consultant thought that the meeting had gone well. He had no idea that he had insulted anyone. He was merely answering a straightforward question and offered his professional assessment of the quality of their systems.

It is very common for a geek to confuse facts and opinions and to have a tin ear for the response to his statements. Regardless of how smart geeks are, it's important to keep an eye out for statements that substitute opinions for facts.

Judgment Is Swift and Merciless

Geeks generally don't suffer fools gladly. They have busy schedules, tight deadlines, and high standards. First impressions count a lot. Because they value quickness of mind, they tend to judge rather quickly and harshly whether a coworker, subordinate, or even a boss is worthy of respect.

When geeks perceive that someone in their work environment is ineffective due to incompetence or aberrant behavior, they have a tendency to dismiss that person completely. In his book *The Dynamics of Software Development*, Jim McCarthy refers to this phenomenon as *flipping the Bozo Bit.*

When someone has flipped the Bozo Bit on someone, he has changed his opinion of that person's usefulness from a 1 to a 0—that is, completely worthless. In fact, nothing about that other person has actually changed; only the geek's opinion of that person is new. A geek who has decided that someone else is a Bozo tends to build barriers to communication, collaboration, and even to code. Geeks protect themselves and their work from the influence of the Bozo.

In these cases, there tends to be no subtle middle ground. Someone is viewed as either a complete Bozo or a useful contributor. They're either all good or all bad. Geeks generally aren't interested in teasing apart the complexity of another person's strengths or weakness and how to leverage or mitigate them. They just want to judge and move on.

My Work, My Art

Geekwork is all about art. As each technical problem is solved, each network designed, or each program module coded, a tiny piece of art is born. To the observer, these creations may seem simple and straightforwardly mechanical—even boring—but to the creator, the systems integrator or programmer, they are children—tiny extensions of self.

It is important to recognize the differences in how people view work. Most managers think nothing about criticizing a piece of software: "It's too slow." "The interface makes no sense." "No one can use it." These are valid criticisms of most software, but the speaker has to realize how such things are heard, not how they are said. The same manager would never think about looking at someone's newborn child and saying, "What an ugly baby." Even if a baby is ugly, we instinctively spare the feelings of new parents with something like, "That's going to be one smart kid" or "He looks like you." Just as parents take criticism of their child personally, geeks take criticism of their art personally.

On the plus side, the beauty and utility of their work is a great source of pride for most geeks. They put extraordinary effort into the creative solution of a technical or business problem.

Geek Smarts

Geeks share a reverence for smart people, or at least for smart geeks. They hold those with creativity, knowledge, ideas, and the ability to apply them in very high esteem. That doesn't mean that geeks love all smart people. They can appreciate someone with great sales skills, but only in a limited way. They bestow deep appreciation only within knowledge communities where all the participants have the ability to recognize true genius.

Those who have deep knowledge about their field of endeavor, are able to apply it to real-world projects, and are willing to share their gifts are considered technical leaders. This type of leadership is not only valuable for respect and influence. The strength of technical leadership on a project can make the difference between the success and failure of the entire team.

Although top-notch technicians are typically held in high regard, they can lose the respect of their peers through condescending, selfish, or disruptive behavior. Occasionally, some of the best geeks end up ostracized by their peers, reviled by their users, and dismissed from their jobs. How does this happen? They lose their positions through rude and condescending behavior or refusal to share their wisdom with peers.

Several times in my career, I've had to fire people of immense intelligence and technical ability. Firing them seemed like an incredible waste of talent, but they had proved themselves either

incapable of or unwilling to modify their behaviors to become productive members of their project teams. No matter how smart,
capable, and creative they were, their net contributions to their
projects were negative due to their impact on others.

Loyalty to Technology and Profession

In almost every consulting assignment that I have undertaken, I
hear the complaint at one point or another that the "technical people" aren't loyal to the business. They have high turnover rates and
frequently jump from company to company. They are variously
accused of being incapable, disinterested, or intransigent.

My typical response is, "Duh. What would you expect?" (or
something a bit more polite). The clue is right there in the name
itself: *technical people*. The word *technical* finds it roots in the same
soil as the word *technique*. These are people who are more captivated by technique than by application. Their attention is more
engaged by how a system works rather than what a system does. You
can't expect that they will respond to a situation in the same way
that others would. When they are confronted with a broken computer, the puzzle of why it's not working is probably more exciting
than how much money the organization is losing due to the failure.

Of course, this is exactly the opposite response of the typical
business executive. Most businesspeople are much more concerned
about how much the company is losing or the operational impact
of a systems failure. This is not to say that geeks don't care about
business, but it does run a strong second to technique.

Geeks don't see themselves as disloyal. If you ask them about
how often they change careers, they will tell you that they never
have even if they held jobs with three companies in three different
industries in the past five years. They may have changed jobs, but
they probably haven't changed technologies. Would a carpenter say
that he had changed careers because he changed construction companies?

The company or industry is not how geeks identify themselves. People generally identify themselves based on their membership in a group of some sort. This self-identification is made based on membership in a company, industry, profession, or technology. If asked at a dinner party what one does for a living, the answer is usually based on one of these categories. "I work for Microsoft," or "I'm in insurance," or "I'm a lawyer," or "I'm a network analyst."

Since the primary orientation for geeks is toward technique, that provides the foundation for their strongest group identification. They are most loyal to their selected group, which is generally based on technology or service delivery method. This is where they are most comfortable. For example, a typical Java developer will be more interested in sharing thoughts, ideas, and concerns with Java developers from another company than with a salesperson from his own company. Or an independent contractor who provides software testing services will be more concerned with talking to other contractors than to marketing people from a current client.

Geeks can develop an attachment to a company or an industry, but it will occur only when there is a strong corporate or industry culture.

Money and Fairness

Geeks are generally not captivated by money. It's not that they're uninterested in money; it's just not the primary motivator. Money can be very important to them, but not for the common reasons. Most people who are motivated by money are driven by the power, position, prestige, or possessions that money brings. Geeks not only are generally not interested in these things; they tend to look down on those who are.

Their attitudes toward money are much more tied up in their strong sense of fairness and justice. No one wants to feel taken advantage of; everyone wants to feel fairly compensated for their value. The passion for reason combines with a strong belief in meritocracy to create an atmosphere where money is a primary measure of the value that one delivers to the organization.

When I first became responsible for setting salaries for a group of geeks, I made the typical managerial assumption about employee ideas about money: no matter how much you make, you always want more. (Everyone has an insatiable appetite for more money.) I also assumed that my job was to try to match the value that an individual brought to the organization with that person's salary.

Generally, this assumption worked well. Then I had to deal with Bob's salary. I was only twenty-eight years old, and Bob was in his mid-sixties (geeks are not necessarily in their twenties and thirties.) He had been with the company for almost thirty years and was a loyal contributor. In the late 1970s, he had been a pioneer in the application of microprocessors and had one of the keenest technical minds around. But Bob was on the tail end of his career. No longer in the forefront of technology, he also lacked the energy to keep up with the demanding schedule of consulting.

My difficulty was that his salary had risen quite high during the days of his peak productivity, and I couldn't in good conscience give him a raise when he was already making much more money than some others who contributed more.

I agonized for days how to discuss this with him. How could I tell him that I couldn't give him a raise? I didn't want to hurt his feelings, and I didn't want him to feel that the company didn't value all his years of loyal service. Finally, I couldn't avoid it any longer and set up an appointment to meet with him. Even walking into the meeting room, I was still debating how to approach the conversation and dreading hurting his feelings.

Bob must have sensed my agony, because he decided to save me from this uncomfortable situation. He started the conversation: "You don't have to worry. I don't expect a raise. In fact, I can't believe how much money I'm being paid. I'm not where I used to be. In fact, if the company were to ask me to take a pay cut right now, I'd be happy to do it. I don't really deserve this much." With that tension relieved, we proceeded to have a very productive conversation about his performance, and we both left feeling good about the meeting.

I'm not going to suggest that every geek has the self-awareness, honesty, and integrity that Bob demonstrated to me that day, but I do believe that that strong sense of fairness is very common. Although geeks are not unique in their attachment to fairness, their passion for reason heightens this sensibility in the typical geek.

Independence and Rebellion

Although most geeks are relatively timid and quiet people, scratch the surface, and you will find a strong rebellious streak. Don't confuse their natural reserve as passivity. The image of the rebel is strongly rooted in the mythos of individualism, especially American individualism. This rebel image touches on many concepts that geeks hold dear, including freedom, independence, self-determination, integrity, and creativity.

I'm not suggesting that under their typical quiet, calm demeanor, geeks are violent obstructionists, although it can seem that way to harried managers. A few are, but they are the rare exception to the rule. They just have a strong need for independent thought, which requires not following past dogma blindly. They revel in overturning outdated notions in the name of progress. True curiosity cannot be pursued with intellectual integrity without questioning past reasoning. It is not a blind rebellion for the sake of being contrary; it is born of the need for a free inner life of thought and reason.

Because this rebellious sensibility is so deeply rooted in the beliefs of most geeks, cross it at your own peril. What may seem an insignificant request for conformity, such as a request that a geek wear a coat and tie to a client meeting, can be met with what seems a disproportionate and impassioned response. Repeated disregard of their sensibility can easily result in a mutiny. More than once I've seen project teams rise up and reject a manager. The rebellious spirit combined with the lack of respect for imposed hierarchy (discussed in the next chapter) can lead to astounding consequences.

Summary

FUNDAMENTAL QUESTIONS

- What makes geeks different from other employees?
- What's special about their interests, values, and behaviors?

KEY IDEAS

- There are lots of stereotypes about geeks, and many of them are true.
- Geeks bring nontraditional values and interests to the workplace.
- These unique characteristics are important to how geeks respond to work, power, and leadership.
- These characteristics form the foundation for a geek subculture within the larger organizational structure.

3

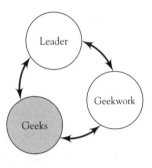

Groups of Geeks

If you want to lead geeks, it's not enough to understand them as individuals. That would be like trying to understand the character of an entire city by looking at only one living room. You've got to extend your understanding of the individual to encompass how group dynamics affects the attitudes and behavior of geeks in the workplace.

Geeks rarely work solo. The complexity and scope of geekwork is now so large that most projects include anywhere from a handful to thousands of geeks. How these professionals interact with each other has profound implications for those who would lead them.

Geek Work Culture

We all have some notion of what work culture is, but no two people may agree how to describe the culture of a particular working group.

The scholar Edgar Schein has formulated a theory that organizational culture develops over time as groups share experiences of encountering problems and solving them. As the group members collectively experiment with differing responses to similar situations, they develop shared assumptions about their environment. Together, they learn what works and what doesn't, leading to the development of shared assumptions that become so embedded in the group's identity that the members act on them without being able to articulate their foundational beliefs. In all work environments, those shared assumptions are affected by the personalities of the group members, the nature of the work, the competitive environment, the organizational structure, and the style of the managers.

Based on my observations, the most important factor affecting the culture in geek groups seems to be the personality and management style of the immediate group leader. These groups are very sensitive to the leadership style of their most present manager, resonating with the personality of the leader. If the manager tightly controls information, the group doesn't communicate. If the manager shows no sense of urgency, the organization ambles along at a comfortable pace.

My own theory, admittedly untested, is that these groups are so sensitive to leadership style because the work itself does not impose a specific structure that mitigates the effects of personality. In a manufacturing plant, the organizational culture would also be affected by the style of leadership, but to a much lesser extent. The need to move physical materials from one place to another and to assemble things in a specific order would also imprint itself on the assumptions shared by the line workers. In most geekwork, there are few physical necessities that imprint themselves so strongly on the culture.

Geek Subculture

Although larger organizations may have a single culture, the unifying culture tends to be made up of a collection of different subcultures with both common and conflicting assumptions. In organizations where geeks don't represent the dominant culture, they often become a subculture unto themselves, adopting individual attitudes and values, as well as those of the broader technological community.

No matter how much it may seem so, geek subcultures are not completely isolated from the mainstream culture of most organizations. They do adopt many of the values and attitudes common in other functional areas. But there are limits. Where assumptions from the broader culture directly conflict with common attitudes among geeks, differing values will often be ignored or rejected.

How integrated the geek subculture is with the larger community depends on many factors. Physical isolation, mutual antagonism, and controlling management tend to limit geeks' exposure to and adoption of cultural assumptions. Regular communication, cross-functional working teams, and attention from top management help align geek assumptions with those of the general community.

Ambivalence About Groups

In general, geeks are rather ambivalent about joining groups. As introverts, they're most comfortable working alone, concentrating on problems small enough to be attacked by only one person. Our educational system tends to reinforce these tendencies toward isolation. Geeks come to the workforce after spending many years in school, where rewards are handed out for individual work. Over and over again, they're subjected to warnings about plagiarism and collaboration as punishable offenses. Then they come to the workplace, where collaboration and copying are considered virtues rather than vices. Learning to overcome these early lessons in isolation can be difficult for geeks, especially early in their careers.

At the same time, geeks feel attraction for project teams, where there are opportunities to learn from one another, work on complex problems, and gain the recognition of peers. The prospect of joining with other geeks can be almost irresistible.

As a leader, you should recognize these conflicting impulses and how they may affect the formation of project teams. These tensions can lead to a number of challenges to forming effective groups, including teams that never really form as teams, individuals who isolate themselves from others, or fracturing of teams into hostile factions.

Attitudes Toward Procedures and Policies

Groups of geeks often believe that they are or should be exempted from rules, procedures, or routines that are prescribed for others in the organization. For example, geeks constantly resist office dress codes. They can come up with any number of reasons that they shouldn't have to dress the same way as others in the company do.

Because geekwork is so different from ordinary work, geeks often assume that policies designed for others shouldn't apply to them. They feel that because their work is so abstract and nonroutine, they should not be subject to rules meant to govern more routine work.

Reinforcing this view, geeks have an emotional commitment to the images and values of the rebel. The nonconformism and individualism represented in the loner rebel image is ironically often carried over to the group attitudes and values as well. So instead of adopting the attitude that an individual is an outsider who is special and not subject to others' rules, the entire group begins to view itself as outsiders subject to their own higher laws. This tendency leads many managers to believe that geeks are arrogant and recalcitrant.

Geek World Culture

Over the past decade, we have been bombarded by talk of globalization, from global trade to global workforces. Some alarmists speak of it as if the Germanic hordes were crossing the hills of Rome. Others seem to believe that it will portend a return to Eden, ushering in an era of unprecedented egalitarianism and access to information.

If you want to see what global work culture looks like, there's no need to wait twenty years to see how things turn out. Just go into any IT department or biotech startup lab. What you will find is truly the melting pot created not by ideology but by technology. While futurists argue whether new technologies will concentrate or decentralize power in the world, the creation of the technology itself has broken down the cultural boundaries in the geek workplace.

Today's technology office draws talent from every corner of the globe. Just as oil companies scour the planet for increasingly more remote and inaccessible sources of black gold, technology companies search the planet for rare engineering talent, engaging almost as much creativity in using these resources as finding them. The chronic shortage of talented workers has resulted in two distinct patterns of work globalization: the melting pot office and the virtual office.

In the melting pot office, geeks from every corner of the world congregate to form project teams, departments, and companies. In almost any U.S.-based company's IT department, you will find software developers from the United States, Canada, India, China, Russia, Eastern Europe, Western Europe, Australia, and Africa. Listening in on a project team meeting might feel like eavesdropping on a conversation in the hallway at the United Nations. This sort of diversity brings with it many challenges. Individual conflict, miscommunication, and cliquish subgroups often arise during projects with language barriers, as do differing cultural assumptions and work styles.

In the virtual office, individuals or groups of geeks are dispersed across the globe but connected through e-mail, instant messaging, videoconferencing, databases, and other electronic collaboration tools. Individuals may work together on many projects simultaneously or over a period of years without ever meeting each other. The challenges of creating intellectual property collectively with people you've never met shouldn't be underestimated, but the scarcity of talent and the value of technology are driving geekwork into ever more complicated global organizational structures.

While the virtual office and the melting pot office are forging a new global work culture, our imaginations are also being stretched with new and more complicated forms of employer and employee relationships. The same forces that have created the global geek-work culture have also created outsourcing, contracting, independent contracting, project consultants, body shops, and global recruiting firms.

Note that geeks are often accused of being direct, blunt, or even insensitive in their communication with others. Often, it's true. But it's not because they're social misfits; rather, it's an outgrowth of the polyglot geek world culture. Since many of the people in the workplace speak English as a second language, they tend to stick to the facts, blunt and direct as they may sound. Over time, it has become embedded in the culture. Expect geeks to be direct, and don't take it personally.

Democracy at Work

Just as geeks have absorbed the romance and mythology of individualism, they've also come to embrace the ideas of democracy and to expect it in their work environments. Many of the core assumptions that have become popular in civic culture have now been transported into the geek workplace. Such ideas as one man–one vote, representative democracy, and majority rule challenge the assumptions of many managers about the nature of power and influence in organizations.

Over the past hundred years of managerial history, most organizations have adopted notions of hierarchy, power, and command and control from a military management model in which authority is vested in a single individual at the top of a hierarchy, and powers are delegated downward in limited ways. The legitimacy of the person at the top is derived from governmental, charismatic, or economic power.

In this traditional model, the worker-manager relationship is defined by the distribution of power and proximity to the top of the organizational pyramid. Here, power is conceptualized as a zero-sum commodity to be wrested from one another in an adversarial contest. Authority granted by managers through delegation or lost to managers through collective bargaining is gained by workers, and vice versa.

Especially at the team level, geeks frequently reject this sort of authoritarian control and demand a voice in the goals, measures, and means of their work groups. They come to the workplace with expectations that are fundamentally different from those of non-geeks.

The drive for democratic and open decision making does not have to result in power clashes with the managerial hierarchy in the organization if you can separate the need to control the ends of geekwork from the means. Managing the goals of a group—the ends—tends to be much less controversial than trying to control the means of day-to-day work.

Meritocracy at Work

Geeks are a competitive lot. Most have been rewarded early in life for their technical prowess with attention, money, and apprecia-tion. Most geeks transport the assumptions about rewards and recognition from academia into the workplace.

As a student in the academic world, success is largely based on individual performance. "I got an A on my test." "My paper got the highest score in the class." "I had the highest GPA in my graduat-ing class." Most awards are issued based on individual academic achievement or athletic ability.

The background of success as an individual producer combines with the attitudes about democracy to form a solid foundational assumption about the nature of meritocracy at work. Geeks assume that all areas of life, especially the work environment, should con-form to a strict hierarchy of merit. Since the nature of their work immediately following graduation feels like an extension of their academic career, they naturally assume that the standards for suc-cess are the same.

Unfortunately, these assumptions are not always compatible with the real-world workplace. Although individual merit is, or at least should be, a contributing factor in the doling out of recognition and rewards, it is not the only thing that should be considered. It can't be. The assumptions about meritocracy become problems for both individual geeks and groups of geeks in two distinct ways.

The first major problem with this assumption surfaces when geeks disagree on the measures of individual success. Because they tend to see the world through technology-colored lenses, they often believe that the only valid criterion on which merit should be measured is technical knowledge. Not productivity. Not managerial skills. Not communication skills. When promotions, bonuses, or awards are bestowed on those who excel at things that geeks devalue, they feel that the organization has violated its commitment to meritocracy, and they are outraged.

Another problem with the idea of pure meritocracy arises when geeks work on project teams. The belief that rewards should be, and will be, handed out based strictly on individual merit can lead to inappropriate behavior. When a project fails miserably and the organizational result is decidedly negative, it's not uncommon for one team member nevertheless to complain that he didn't get a bonus even though he finished his part on time.

Mania for Play and Pranks

In the popular imagination, geeks are perpetually serious, forever obsessed with technology. Of course, this is an oversimplified view. Geeks love to play. Whether it's puzzles, Dungeons and Dragons, computer games, or foosball, geeks love a good game. They bring that playful sensibility to the workplace too. Even the most serious corporate setting will not deter geeks from getting in a little fun. That fun usually conforms to the other general rules of geek values and behavior, embodying competition, the joy of puzzles, and reverence for smarts. Most often, play takes the form of games and pranks.

Geeks love pranks. They elevate the practical joke to an art form requiring cleverness, careful execution, elaborate planning, and, above all, creativity. The old standbys, like tying someone's shoes together under the lunch table, is way too mundane. A good prank is not only funny and unexpected; it also demonstrates the intelligence and creativity of its perpetrator. Pranks often escalate into competition between individuals and groups, resulting in thematic series.

One of my favorite examples comes from the Massachusetts Institute of Technology, the home of many odd rituals, where few are more amusing than the long tradition of pranks. Every year, students try to outdo one another in the creativity and elaborateness of their gags. One year, the students assembled an entire police car on top of the Great Dome that crowns Baker Engineering Library, complete with flashing lights, wailing siren, and doughnuts on the seat. The following year, the same dome was transformed into a giant beanie cap, with propeller blades twenty feet long.

Since the demise of the dot-coms, play at work has taken a bad rap. It's often joked about as the hallmark of an immature company with no concept of solid business practices. Although play at work may seem like a waste of time on the company clock, be cautious about trying to control it excessively. Try to distinguish between hard-working, dedicated groups blowing off steam and out-of-control, aimless play. Even the most dedicated geeks need to restore their creative energies through play.

My Hierarchy, Your Hierarchy

Although it may seem logical, the pervasive attachment to democracy and meritocracy does not prevent geek groups from having a similarly strong attachment to building hierarchies. The natural need to develop social structures heightened by the geek machismo leads to the creation of hierarchical structures.

All human groups exhibit some form of social structure that provides a context in which everyday life is played out. These structures provide information essential to creating effective group interaction and action, supplying role and status, as well as implied methods for decision making and identification of meaning and purpose.

Unfortunately, this does not manifest itself as you might expect. Work groups have managers, and managers report to executives, and executives report to boards of directors. It should be simple to understand the hierarchy of a work group: the lines of authority are clearly spelled out, and roles and relationships are generally laid out by dictate. So you, as a leader, structure the organization, and assume that you've provided a functional hierarchy that will drive decision making, information flow, and activity coordination. You assume that everyone will respect your choice of manager.

But geeks are notoriously resistant to authority bestowed from outside and generally reject official hierarchies. They tend to build their own based on those values that they hold dear: knowledge and meritocracy. The more technical knowledge one possesses and the more capable one is of applying that knowledge, the higher is that person's social status.

These self-constructed hierarchies generally do not attempt to subvert the official power bestowed by the external organization. To understand the nature of the geek hierarchy, you must view geeks through the lenses of influence and respect rather than power. The technical leader of a group may not hold the official power to make decisions, but nevertheless he holds great sway on the opinions of the others in the group.

If you were to place a camera above the work environment of a technical work group and trace the walking paths of its members throughout the day, you'd find that there are certain places—certain offices or cubicles—that are hubs of activity. These congregating points are the homes of the informal geek leaders. Others are approaching them all day with questions about technology, politics, and life in general.

The occupants of those busy cubicles are influential, if not powerful, people in the organization. Recognize who they are, and be mindful of their position, since they can support or oppose your agenda. Seek advice from these influential geeks. You'll often find that they have attracted the respect of their peers for good reason, including their technical brilliance and sometimes their organizational insight.

Because of this, attempting to pull rank on a group of geeks tends to be counterproductive. Statements like, "I'm the vice president of this company, and you will do as I tell you," tend to elicit stifled giggles rather than trembling fear. Since geeks have little respect for imposed hierarchy, trying to use title or position as an explicit source of authority doesn't work well. They understand your authority but respond much better to explanations than demands justified only by title.

Machismo Everywhere

Collectively, geeks need hierarchies. Individually, they not only need to establish position within that hierarchy, but to establish means to advance within it.

Hierarchies are built on dominance relationships between individuals, and these status relationships confer meaning and roles to members of the groups. Members of the group struggle to acquire positions of choice. In human societies and groups, these struggles historically took place between male competitors, with the outcome based on strength of body or mind, that is, machismo.

For years, geek groups have been bastions of male outsiderness. Although decidedly different from the classic image of the athletic locker room, geek groups have largely been testosterone havens where groups of mostly men compete for dominance based on decidedly nontraditional criteria. It's rare to see IT project meetings where programmers beat their chests and threaten one another, although you will occasionally witness shouting and table pounding. Geeks have developed their own analogues for these behaviors, competing with each other based on signs of high intelligence and only occasionally on the more traditional sources of power like strength, charisma, or attractiveness. Geek machismo is expressed in ways unfamiliar to outsiders.

Here are some of the common methods of establishing dominance:

- One-upmanship, with power established by outdoing competitors, demonstrating superior experience or intellect
- Shouting matches, with dominance demonstrated with decibels
- Snide jokes, with supremacy staked out with irony and deprecatory humor
- Dismissive behavior, with power seized by attempting to demonstrate others' irrelevance

Although the makeup of technology organizations is more balanced between men and women than it used to be, geek groups still bear the mark of their exclusively male past. The blunt language and figurative chest thumping remain.

Summary

FUNDAMENTAL QUESTIONS
- What is special about groups of geeks?
- How are geek group dynamics different from those of other groups?

KEY IDEAS
- Leading geeks requires a clear understanding of the group dynamics of geeks, as well as their individual values and interests.
- Geek culture is a subculture of the organization and adopts many of the characteristics of the wider organization.

- There are some common elements of geek subcultures that a leader should understand: ambivalence about groups, attitudes toward procedures and policies, meritocracy at work, mania for play and pranks, attitudes toward hierarchy, and machismo.

4

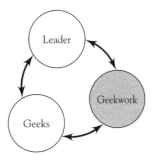

The Nature of Geekwork

The third member of the tripartite relationship is geekwork. Here, organizational culture and individual personalities interact with knowledge work to form an unusual dynamic that often confounds leaders unaccustomed to working with geeks, as well as some who are. The character of geekwork doesn't conform to many common assumptions or images of the workplace, turning some long-held beliefs on their heads. In this chapter, we take a look at some of the unique characteristics and constraints that geekwork imposes on both geeks and leaders. In the next chapter, we examine more closely how geeks perform geekwork.

Failure Is Normal

Let's start with one of the dirty little secrets of geekwork that makes both leaders and geeks uncomfortable: often things don't work out. Projects fail. In fact, lots of projects fail. Every year the Standish Group, a consulting and research firm, studies the outcomes of thousands of software application development projects. Based on an evaluation of its outcome, they classify each project into one of three categories: successful, failed, or challenged. Successful projects were completed on time, within budget, and with all the major functionality completed as originally specified. Failed projects are those that were cancelled before completion. And challenged projects eventually limped over the finish line late, over budget or with major features missing.

In 1998, the Standish Group classified 26 percent of projects as successful and 46 percent as challenged. Twenty-eight percent of projects were classified as complete failures.[1] For those of you who have been a bit distant from geekwork, these may sound like dismal numbers, but the scary thing is how encouraging they are. The fact that 26 percent of projects were classified as successes is a tribute to the progress that the industry is making with geekwork, since it's almost *double* the success rate the group found when it started doing these studies in 1994.

The point here is not that geeks are incompetent or that geekwork is hopeless, but that creativity and innovation are difficult to do and even more difficult to integrate into an organization successfully. Any sort of creative work is difficult and problematic, and you've got to be prepared for that. There's little certainty in geekwork besides uncertainty. It's kind of like stand-up comedy. Even the most hilarious and talented comics report that only about a third of their new jokes work with audiences. They just keep trying new ones, reworking or throwing out those that don't work and keeping the ones that do. Geekwork too is a hit-or-miss business. If you expect every project to be completed on schedule and on budget, you're likely to be constantly disappointed.

Ambiguity Rules

One of the defining features of geekwork is its ambiguity. Most non-geek work is relatively clear: you know what you want to accomplish, you know what you need to do, and you know how to do it. You've just got to get on with it. When you hire a truck driver to take a load of oranges from southern California to Des Moines, Iowa, there's not too much to discuss besides where and when to pick up the oranges, where to drop them off, and how much the job pays. But when you embark on a project of geekwork, there's no such clarity.

There are all sorts of questions that need to be answered before you can get on with the work—for example:

- What do you want to accomplish?
- What problem are you trying to solve, or what opportunity are you trying to exploit?
- Why do you want to do that?
- Who will use the new technology?
- How will the technology interact with the users?
- How will the system look inside?
- What other systems must it interact with?
- How will it interact with other systems?
- What other problems will be introduced by solving this one?
- Once you know what the technology will look like, how should you build it?
- Who will do what work?
- Who will be involved in the process besides the geeks doing the purely technical work?

These kinds of questions go on and on. And although they may seem unnecessary, frustratingly detailed, and annoying to answer, they are critical to the success of any project. A great many failed projects can be traced to failure to clarify these types of issues before starting to implement the technology.

Figuring Out What to Do Can Be Harder Than Doing It

You can think about the ambiguity of geekwork by categorizing all the questions into two fundamental categories:

- What are we going to do?
- How will we do it?

Both categories of questions are critical and hide innumerable ambiguities and difficulties, but in general, the first can be more difficult to answer than the second. Within complex organizations, building a consensus about what should be done can often be harder work than actually doing what you decide to do.

Often, the "What are we going to do?" question is referred to as requirements gathering, as if there are clear and distinct ideas out there, just waiting to be harvested like ripe strawberries in a patch. Everyone knows what's supposed to be done, according to this way of thinking; it just remains to collect that information and write it down. Unfortunately, the reality is usually much more complex and subtle. There are often many ideas about what should be done that conflict, overlap, and mesh with each other. Different factions and interest groups within the organization often have differing agendas and ideas about what they want done or whether they want anything done. Most of the ideas are incompletely formed and have yet to be clearly articulated. All too often, there are ideas about what should be done without any clear purpose or goal. Building a consensus within a community of users can be very difficult political work, not to be dismissed as valueless harvesting of existing information. So don't be surprised when a major part of a project is devoted to discovering what should be done rather than doing it. It's normal and necessary. Building consensus is real work, and it is not to be dismissed or devalued.

Geekwork Is Organized by What You Don't Know

When you stop to think about it, most work is structured by certainty rather than uncertainty. In most sales departments, salespeople are assigned to specifically delineated territories broken down by geography, industry, or even alphabetically. The salespeople are usually told by marketing exactly what products to sell based on a specific set of features, functions, and benefits to differentiate the product from that of competitors. They even know the position of the person whom they should target with the product. In a fast food restaurant, cashiers take orders, collect money, make change, bag selections, and deliver them to customers. It's all very clearly spelled out in their training videos. Work is just as clear for the cooks, the assistant managers, and the managers.

But the organization of geekwork is not dictated by the physical layout of a plant, the flow of materials through a process, or even by the customer interface. Geekwork is structured not by what you know about the nature of the work but by two key factors: what you don't know about the work and the specialized knowledge required to figure out what you don't know.

Every position within a project is centered on figuring out something you don't know. Systems architects focus their energy on trying to figure out how to design a system. When they start designing, they have no idea what it will look like when they're done. They don't simply apply a standard template to a standard problem and come up with a standard answer, as if attaching a bumper to a chassis. There are few interchangeable parts. In fact, when they start a project, they don't even know what problems they are trying to solve. Their first task is to try to figure out what problems to solve. Their jobs are structured not around what they know about the problem at hand, but by their general knowledge of how to ferret out the goals and constraints of systems and then to develop creative designs that meet them.

This structure both encourages and results from geeks' problem-solution mind-set. Because they love puzzles, they gravitate to this sort of work. And because their work is structured around problems and solutions, their problem-solution mind-set is constantly reinforced.

Deep Concentration

One of the great joys of geekwork is that it is fundamentally creative. It requires losing oneself in a problem, focusing thoughts on a small piece of reality, and staying with it for long periods of time. You can't create software or design hardware while thinking about your bank account, your car, or what your children will eat for dinner. The minutiae of everyday life melt away as you focus on only the problem at hand. Time and language stop while you float in a pure world of ideas and experience the joy of puzzles.

If a geek gets interrupted while trying to concentrate on technical work, it's a long journey back to reality. Disruptions to concentration are like awakening from a dream. And as with a dream, it's very difficult to get back and continue where you left off. Depending on the complexity of the work and the depth of concentration, it may take hours to resume productive work after even a brief interruption.

The demands of geekwork are exactly the opposite of most managerial work, which is driven by relationships, free-flowing communication, schedules, and budgets. Managerial work centers around the coordination of resources and people. Time and language never stop; they are the essence of managerial work. Most managerial work is driven by interruption, constantly shifting from topic to topic as individuals and groups compete for time and attention.

It is not surprising that few managers truly understand the importance of concentration to geekwork, and even fewer respect its necessity when interacting with technology professionals. Managers need timely information and rarely worry that their interruptions of subordinates may impede the progress that they are so anxious to measure.

What is more surprising is how few technical managers (many who used to do geekwork themselves) remember how frustrating it is to be interrupted. They thoughtlessly allow the nature of whatever work they are doing to imprint itself on their interactions with others. When doing technical work, they seek isolation. When doing managerial work, they seek constant interaction with those doing technical work.

What Is Work?

For both geeks and managers, one of the most frustrating aspects of geekwork is defining the boundaries of whether one is working. For most jobs, there is some level of ambiguity in deciding when one is working or not working, but it's easier for some than for others. If you work at a grocery store as a cashier and are standing at the register ringing out customers, you're definitely working. If you're counting the cash in the drawer at the end of your shift, you're working. If you're reading sales literature on a new register system that you might recommend to your manager, you're probably working. If you're in the parking lot listening to a customer complain about the service at the store, you may be working. If you're in the shower at home in the morning thinking about how to improve the flow of customers through the store, you're probably not on the clock. There's always some ambiguity, and for geekwork, the boundaries are even harder to define.

If you are a programmer and are sitting at your desk typing code into the system, you're definitely working. If you're at the water cooler discussing a technical problem with a coworker, you're working. If you're at lunch sketching out system architecture on a napkin, you may be working. If you're strolling in the woods thinking deeply about how to connect two systems together, are you working? It's a tough call, but for many, movement and solitude are crucial to the concentration that geekwork demands. Without reflection, much active time may be wasted following unproductive avenues down to dead ends.

In an abstract sense, it's not really important to define, but at a practical level, it may be very important, especially given that so much of technical work is done based on hourly charges. This can make defining work an uncomfortable exercise for both geeks and managers. Not only do managers try to limit the activities that are defined as work, geeks sometimes don't feel comfortable taking the time for the reflection that they need. Many programmers don't feel comfortable that they're working if they're not actively typing coding.

Ironically, when managers try too hard to limit the definition of work, they raise the cost of projects. If geeks are told that they are working only when they are typing, then they are not allowed the necessary time to think and will waste lots of time typing useless code that won't work or will turn out to be creative dead ends.

Remember that geeks deliver most of their value through thought, not behavior, so eliminating thought from the work reduces the value.

Minimize your attempts to govern how geeks work; instead, focus on what should be accomplished. Individuals vary widely in the activities that result in productive work. For some, a long time of creative gestation is followed by a short burst of unbelievable productivity. For some, slow and steady production works better. If you focus on the ends that you want achieved rather than the means, everyone will be happier.

Subordinates Know More Than Managers

Geekwork challenges some of our most cherished beliefs about the nature of work and the organizations in which work takes place. These assumptions do more than order our daily work life. They also have strong ties to our sense of decency and self-worth.

Among the most entrenched ideas challenged by geekwork are those about the relationship between supervisors and subordinates. Although many changes have taken place in the organization of work in the past one thousand years, our attitudes toward the role of a supervisor have changed only modestly. Many of our notions are still rooted in the history of the European medieval guild system. Under the guild system, master craftsmen who had reached a very high proficiency with their work and were able to demonstrate both technical mastery and business success trained other craftsmen in their discipline. Masters were served by journeymen, who had achieved a modest level of expertise under the supervision of their masters. And both masters and journeymen oversaw apprentices, who were beginning their training. The relationship between the master and his subordinates was one of both supervisor and teacher. No one could reach such a lofty level without having mastered all the fine details of apprentice and journeyman's work.

Today, we still harbor the tacit assumption that this system of mastery remains in place—that managers of a group should be the best trained in the craft and that they are responsible for the training of more junior and less knowledgeable subordinates. But as technology has become increasingly complex, specialization has rendered this assumption invalid. In the high-tech world, it is virtually unheard of to find a CEO who started out sweeping the floors and worked his way through every job in the enterprise to reach the top of the company. The range of technology makes it impossible for anyone to know all the details about even one system, let alone know everything about an entire company.

In geekwork, the traditional knowledge distribution assumed in the guild system is completely turned on its head. Managers rarely know all the details about the work of their subordinates. It's not possible, and it is not necessarily desirable. Management of technical teams has become a specialty unto itself.

The inversion of this unspoken assumption, commonly held by both geeks and managers, leads both to discomfort. Managers feel compelled to try to make technical decisions about issues that they are not equipped to handle. Technicians refuse to acknowledge or respect the expertise that managers bring to the organization, since it is different from their own. Ultimately, both managers and geeks strain against this outmoded idea.

My Work, Our Work

The challenges inherent in geekwork include some unanswerable riddles that bedevil professionals throughout their careers. Among them is the irreconcilable tension between the need to work alone and the need to work with others.

The most visible manifestation of this dialectic appears in personal time management. Individual geeks must strike a balance between time alone to focus on production and time for both formal and informal coordination with others. Too often, that balance is struck based on personal comfort rather than the demands of a specific project or team. Introverts tend to place more value on solitude, and extroverts tend toward collaboration and coordination.

But this competition for focus between the collective and the individual runs much deeper than just governing personal time allocation. There is also an emotional component that hearkens back to childhood, to the educational system, that so often imprints itself on adults in ways they never suspect. The academic culture of individual success leaves a lasting impression on the psyche of geeks that they struggle with throughout their professional careers. Grades, awards, and scholarships all reinforce the value of personal production, and the competitive machismo of geeks is right at home on the intellectual battlefield. But success in the work environment is primarily a group affair in which everyone wins or loses together. If decisive portions of a technical project are not completed, success on subsections of the system is irrelevant.

Nevertheless, many geeks consider themselves successful if their part of a system is completed. Someone who sees others on a project struggling may take pleasure in triumph, in proof of individual superiority, rather than help out. If their individual piece of work is built and functioning to their satisfaction, then they feel that their contribution is complete. Even if it doesn't connect with the rest of a system, they nevertheless feel finished and relieved of responsibility for ensuring that their work smoothly integrates with that of others. The tension between individual contribution and group success constantly challenges teams.

The Problem with Problems

Geeks love problems. Whether puzzles, philosophical conundrums, math problems, or broken machines, geeks find comfort, validation, excitement, and joy in solving problems.

Problems provide more than just motivation and amusement; they have become the primary organizing metaphor driving geekwork. Every plan, every activity is conceptualized as a solution to a problem. In this model, problems become the initiators of action; without problems, nothing happens. This problem-solution worldview dictates that technology be designed to resolve technical or business problems or to exploit opportunities (which are also conceptualized as problems).

Marketing literature provides the most unmistakable evidence of this phenomenon where the word *solution* has now joined the pantheon of the overused hyperbolic phrase. It's no longer acceptable to call a product a product. Every product is now pitched as some sort of solution. Slogans like "Bimbah, your e-mail solution" or "Symacule, your database solution" are thrown about, begging the consumer to ask, "A solution to what?" The answer is, "To some problem that you may not even know you have."

Although I poke fun at the marketing abuse of the problem-solution model, it has proved to be a robust and useful approach to technical management. For geekwork that is inherently ambiguous and difficult to define, problems offer relatively clear direction and boundaries. Out of all the possible things that one might do in a day, solving a particular problem provides focus and urgency to work and helps to prioritize tasks.

But like all other metaphors, problem-solution has limits and problems of its own. The model is very sensitive to the quality of problem formulation. A solution can only be as good as its problem. If problems are not carefully selected, well defined, and articulately communicated, the solution developed will be of limited value. If you ask a bad question, you'll get a bad answer.

In addition, problems carry emotional baggage, toting along negative connotations wherever they go. If you've got a problem, something's wrong. There's an implied inadequacy or failure that's occurred somewhere. The pervasive negativism can contribute to the cynicism that's so common in technical groups.

Perhaps the most troubling problem with problems is that some essential geekwork cannot be represented in the model. Not all work can be conceptualized in such a linear way. In the problem-solution worldview, work occurs in a clear sequence: identify a problem, solve the problem, and then move on to the next problem.

Problems can exist in only one of two states: solved or not solved. Once a problem is solved and its solution implemented, you're done. Resolved problems don't require attention.

Many things in life don't really work that way. But to geeks, work that doesn't cleanly conform to the model is rejected, devalued, or forced to conform inappropriately. For example, most human relationship issues aren't easily represented in this format. Relationships require ongoing communication, negotiation, and dispute resolution. You can't just ignore a business relationship until some problem develops. It must be maintained. Some things need to be managed on an ongoing basis and can't be reduced in this way.

One of the most common expressions of the limits of the problem-solution conceptualization of geekwork is the initiative that's launched whenever an operational issue or limitation is discovered. Frequently, these are attempts to apply the problem-solution approach to a human problem that doesn't lend itself to these types of one-time resolution. For example, most geek groups have occasional spasms of activity to try to improve communication or quality. They put together a team to oversee the initiative, hold meetings, plan seminars, build technical infrastructure, and encourage information sharing. But invariably these efforts lose energy and die from neglect. The ongoing work of maintaining these efforts doesn't conform to the problem-solution model and is invariably abandoned when a new problem arises that conforms better and seems more urgent.

Done Is Hard to Do

In geekwork, done is very hard to do. On the surface, it seems that finishing a project should be simple. In the problem-solution world, you are done when the problem is solved. But in practice, the only project teams that have no problem distinguishing "almost done" from "done" are the ones that never even come close to finishing. For those that do try to reach closure, figuring out what *done* really means is quite difficult and requires hard choices made with incomplete information. With no physical reality to indicate completion, it becomes a political decision.

The ambiguity arises out of four distinct and opposing constraints on technical work. The first demand is that a technology solves the problem it set out to address: that it provide a sufficient scope of features to satisfy its requirements. But it's never completely clear what represents the minimum acceptable set of features.

The second constraint is quality: that the technology be delivered at a sufficient level of reliability that its features can be used to solve the problem that it seeks to resolve. In every project, scope and quality must be balanced and compromised in order to complete the work. But measuring quality is difficult and often subjective.

The third constraint is budgetary. Projects frequently overrun budgets, and toward the end, it's never really clear how much more money will be needed to finish. Due to the ambiguity in other factors, budget estimates are rarely right.

The final, and often the most important, constraint is time. Competitive business pressures or regulatory requirements often weigh heavily on the schedule of a project. But toward the end of projects, the irreconcilable demands frequently lead to rather animated discussions about when done is done.

Declaring a project complete ultimately becomes less a technical decision and more a political one about striking the appropriate balance between the competing demands for quality, budget, schedule, and scope. A project is done when the managers concerned forge a consensus that the project is complete and that the constraints have been balanced in accord with overall organizational goals.

One of the most challenging parts of building the consensus of completion is establishing whether the problem has been solved. This difficulty usually goes beyond just establishing whether the technical scope is sufficient. Toward the end of a project, it often becomes clear that the problem that was intended to be addressed was, at the outset, inadequately understood or, worse, unstated.

Establishing whether you have solved an ill-defined problem is nearly impossible.

Finishing a project requires intense commitment and significant effort, so select final deadlines carefully. If you ask a group to push hard to meet a date and work long hours, ignoring their families and forgoing personal interests, don't change that date for anything short of a disaster. If a group makes the extraordinary effort to meet a deadline and you change it without a very good reason, that group will never again commit to meeting a date. They may give lip-service to deadlines but won't truly sign on for what it takes to meet one.

You Can't Control Creativity

Many of the constraints that geekwork imposes on leaders and geeks stem from the fact that it is fundamentally creative, innovative work that cannot be controlled in the traditional sense. Inspiration rarely works on a schedule, rarely arrives at the exact moment that the project plan prescribes, and can't be hurried, pressured, or "incentivized." Innovations can't be scheduled, and insight can't be managed. Although they call it computer science, most geekwork looks more like art than science.

For most leaders, the inability to control the work of subordinates proves frustrating. This is usually the same for managers from both technical and nontechnical backgrounds. They feel out of control, insecure, or incompetent, none of which is conducive to becoming an effective leader. Some respond by pressuring geeks to try to answer questions that they simply can't answer honestly, like, "When are you going to know how to solve this problem?" A geek who hasn't even identified what the flaw is with a system has no idea when it will be fixed, but many managers don't feel comfortable not knowing. Others respond by deciding that since they're "in charge," they will dictate the answer to the unanswerable questions: "I'll just tell the users that the database will be back up at noon."

Both of these approaches may make managers delude themselves into believing that they have control of the geekwork, but all they've really accomplished is forcing a rift between themselves and geeks.

The real source of the problem isn't that the manager isn't in control, but that he assumes it is his job to do so. As long as a leader believes that he can control geekwork, the inherently uncontrollable, he's going to be swimming upstream, fighting reality.

Estimates Are Always Wrong

Just as innovation and creativity are inherently uncontrollable, they are also inherently inestimable. You probably wouldn't expect a meaningful answer to the question, "How long will it take you to reconceptualize our entire business model and transform the organization?" So why would you expect one for the question, "How long will it take you to figure out and implement a completely new way for our customers to look at their order history?"

It's not that geeks don't want to give good estimates. Most often, they really would like to answer the question, not just for the sake of placating a manager, but because they want to know too. Who wouldn't want to know how long their work will take to finish? In fact, many will confidently tell you that they know exactly how long their work will take, and they believe they do. Unfortunately, their confidence is no measure of the quality of an estimate. It is, however, a good yardstick for measuring the depth of their self-delusion. No one can ever really know; they can only guess or lie. If they were working on an assembly line that ran at a fixed speed, they could calculate a good estimate, but geekwork just doesn't work that way. It's not subject to such simple analysis.

The typical response is to try to perform a detailed work breakdown and estimate small bits of work, then to combine them into a single total. This is a sound start, but don't let the detail fool you. Detailed estimates are just detailed lies. They are no more or less lies than less detailed ones. They're still wrong, not because someone's deliberately lying, but because estimates for geekwork are always wrong.

You can look at the project success rates that I cited at the beginning of the chapter in another way too. That 26 percent of projects are now completed successfully may not mean that projects are being managed better, only that estimates are getting better. It also may be that so few are successful not because they are managed poorly but because they are consistently underestimated.

Here are some thoughts on estimating geekwork:

- *The earlier in the process you want an estimate, the further off it'll be.* As projects progress and ambiguity decreases, the accuracy of estimates improves. Trying to force geeks into committing to estimates early in projects doesn't work. They don't know (and they can't know).

- *Estimates from younger geeks are generally further from the truth from those with more experience.* Younger people tend to have a narrower view of what it takes to complete geekwork.

- *Metaphors matter.* Too often, nontechnical managers try to understand geekwork by forming a mental model that compares it to some other sort of work, like manufacturing or construction. These don't work and usually lead to more problems than they solve. The ambiguity and uncertainty of geekwork are qualitatively and quantitatively different from any other form of work. Poor metaphors attempt to gloss over the differences and diminish understanding of the work at hand rather than clarify it. There is no such thing as a software factory.

- *Doubling doesn't work.* One of the most popular ways to estimate projects is to have geeks give managers an estimate and then the manager just doubles it. It's a clean rule of thumb, but applying deterministic mathematical functions to the inherently unknowable doesn't give you any more information than you started out with. And the feeling that you know when you actually don't can be more dangerous than just admitting you don't know.

Summary

FUNDAMENTAL QUESTIONS

- What makes geekwork different from other work?
- What does geekwork demand of geeks and leaders?

KEY IDEAS

- Geekwork is highly abstract and ambiguous.
- Geekwork imposes its own characteristics and constraints on both leaders and geeks.
- Geek leaders must adjust their expectations to account for the nature of geekwork.
- Failure in geekwork is much more common than in other forms of work.
- With geekwork, figuring out what to do can be more difficult than doing it.
- Geekwork often requires deep concentration, with significant blocks of uninterrupted time.
- Geekwork challenges many of our long-held assumptions about hierarchy, since subordinates usually know more about their work than their managers do.
- No matter how hard anyone tries, estimates for how long geekwork will take and cost are always wrong.

5

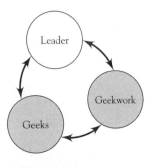

Performing Geekwork

When we turn to the subject of how geeks perform geekwork, the dynamics of the tripartite relationship are played out as geeks and leaders attempt to add value to their organizations through the completion of geekwork.

It's easy, at least in a simplistic sense, to visualize how a worker on a manufacturing line adds value to the product on which he or she is working. A half-built automobile chassis passes the workstation of a factory worker. The worker grabs a bumper from the bucket of bumpers and bolts it onto the moving car. The value-added that the worker has performed was the selection and installation of a bumper. It's very concrete and easy to visualize.

The value-added of knowledge work is not so easily understood. Measuring individual productivity in geekwork can be very difficult. Whether you are looking at the contribution of one programmer to a product development project, or of one postdoctoral researcher attempting to synthesize a chemical for the production of a new drug, it's very difficult to understand the actual value of one person's contribution.

Let's take software development as an example. Over the years, many attempts have been made to measure the complexity of software and the productivity of software developers, such as counting lines of code or the function points. Most are simplistic at best and insulting to the programmer at worst. The challenge in evaluating programmer productivity is that although a program may resemble a bunch of simple text (like typing) or a bunch of pieces that fit together (like the car), it's really a creative product, like a book or painting. No one in any field has ever been able to speed up the creative process, although there are certainly ways to encourage creativity. Nor has the software industry itself been able to come up with an acceptable measure. Most measures tend to miss the subtlety of what geeks do and the true nature of the value they bring to projects and organizations. This leaves you, the manager, with a dilemma: If you can't directly measure geeks' contribution, how can you judge the value delivered? This is not an easy question to answer.

In fact, the ways that geeks add value are so subtle that many of the most successful ones don't even consciously know how they do it. Based on years of observing what works and what doesn't, I have developed a model that I use to describe and evaluate the quality of a geek's work. It is based on a system of twelve competencies.

A competency, loosely defined, is a single facet of one's ability to deliver results. It represents a dimension of one's ability to apply both knowledge and behavior to affect the outcome of a task or project positively.

Note that I say both knowledge *and* behavior. Most geeks (and many managers) place a high value on knowledge (the possession of information either technical or nontechnical) and intelligence (the basic ability to reason). Behavior, however, also plays a role in success, although a lesser one than in other types of work.

Knowledge and intelligence alone are not enough. You probably know one or two really smart geeks who can't seem to complete a job. Some see too many possibilities or threats and are paralyzed with contingencies. Some are obsessed with the perfection of their complex and beautiful visions, forever unsatisfied with the messiness of reality. Others do perfect work, so long as no one—including pesky customers!—"bothers" them.

The missing piece, of course, is behavioral skills, including good communication and teamwork skills. These skills are a crucial part of a competency. However, like knowledge, they are not sufficient in and of themselves. I've worked with many project managers who are superb listeners, great writers, and have hearts of gold—and were completely incapable of meeting a scheduled delivery date. Mastering a competency requires a balance of skills and behaviors that enable performance.

The twelve essential competencies that you can use to measure and guide the productivity of geeks are listed in order of increasing difficulty and complexity. Generally, the ones later in the list are more important as a geek progresses in his or her career.

The Twelve Competencies

1. Technical competence

2. Personal productivity

3. Ability to juggle multiple tasks simultaneously

4. Ability to describe the business context of technical work

5. Ability to forge compromises between business and technical constraints

6. Ability to manage client relationships

7. Ability to manage technical teams

8. Ability to play positive politics

9. Ability to help expand client relationships

10. Ability to work through others, to make others productive

11. Ability to manage ambiguity

12. Ability to manage time horizons

Competency 1: Technical Competence

This competency is the easiest to understand and usually the first one to come to mind when evaluating the value of a geek. When speaking of a geek, someone asks you, "How good is Joe?" This usually means, "How is Joe technically?"

Technical competence consists of two parts: technical breadth indicates a geek's degree of relevant general technical knowledge; technical depth is his specific knowledge about a particular technical subject. Both are important. For example, if Sandy knows how to program stored procedures for Oracle but doesn't know how to do it for any other database, her breadth is very narrow. If she knows how to architect multitiered applications for the Web but doesn't understand transactions, she has moderate breadth, since she has mastered a midlevel range of knowledge. If she can design a complete enterprisewide system that weaves together multiple client platforms, mainframes, application server farms, and several databases, her breadth is extraordinary.

Note the use of the word *relevant*. Lots of geeks are knowledge sponges and are capable of enthralling you with jargon. You, the manager, are at a disadvantage here, since you probably don't know the same topics in depth. More than one manager has been snowed, however, by geeks of seemingly endless expertise, and only later did it surface that the expertise was either irrelevant to the project at hand or not as deep as the manager was led to believe.

Technical depth indicates specialist knowledge of a narrower area to a degree beyond that which would be known by a generalist. As opposed to breadth, depth indicates the ability to navigate the most intricate structures of a small range of technology. If Sandy has spent six weeks as a SQL Server database administrator, she probably knows the basics of the product. If she has spent five years with the product as an aggressive developer who regularly pushes the envelope and is constantly looking for ways to squeeze every ounce of performance out of the system, she probably has a strong depth of knowledge about the product.

Together, breadth and depth measure a geek's technical competence, that is, his or her ability to design and evaluate technical solutions. Remember, however, that great technical skills by themselves are no guarantee of significant contributions to a project.

One factor contributing to the overemphasis on technical skills is training. Nearly all geek education is aimed at improving technical breadth and depth, while very little is devoted to the other half of the coin: the behavioral and team skills. Moreover, the emphasis in many technical training classes, especially those aimed at helping the student get certified in a certain product or technology, is often on acquiring raw knowledge and not on how to apply that knowledge to solve actual problems. Many geeks themselves, including some of the best, disdain the certification classes as useless, or useful mostly for marketing reasons or to appease the boss or the customer.

I'm not suggesting that enhancing technical breadth or depth is a bad idea. It's necessary to keep up with the changes in the technology, but doing so at the expense of developing other competencies could be fatal to a geek's career—and to the success of your project.

Competency 2: Personal Productivity

Personal productivity is another measure of the value of work performed. It's not about the sophistication of the work, just the raw bulk produced by a geek's individual efforts. Peak performers are usually able to complete large volumes of work in reasonable periods of time. It's rare that anyone complains that an IT professional is working too fast, too long, or too hard.

Some geeks write code, some develop technical specifications, some build project plans, some create test plans, and some answer user questions over the telephone. All geeks, however, create deliverables that should further the cause of the organization, and these deliverables can be counted and evaluated.

Personal productivity is strictly related to the speed and quality with which these deliverables are created. The more productive a geek is, the more of these tasks he or she can complete acceptably in a given period of time.

Productive geeks have developed a style and habits that are compatible with their personality. There is no one right way to become a big producer. Some people work in spurts, with short periods of extraordinary productivity followed by slower periods. Others never have those glowing moments of brilliance, but are measured and persistent in their work habits. Like the story of the tortoise and the hare, slow and steady wins the race for some. Then there are the rare few who deliver high energy consistently. They are not to be held up as an example to berate other geeks, but simply supported. Even they have ups and downs, but their productivity swings typically happen on the timescale of months or years rather than hours or days.

Many managers try to force geeks into being productive in the style that the manager is comfortable with rather the one that is appropriate for the geek. This can be disastrous. As a manager and leader, you must develop sensitivity to each geek's personality and production style and help each one discover his own best way to produce. It's important that they (and you) understand that there is no one right way to be productive.

Early geek career development is largely based on enhancing the first two competencies: technical knowledge and personal productivity. At some point in midcareer, improvements in these competencies bring diminishing returns primarily because of the limits of personal productivity. Failure on the part of either the geek or his or her manager to recognize this fact often results in frustration and pain. After years of positive feedback and rewards for improvements in these first two competencies, the accolades stop and careers plateau. Moving beyond this barrier requires changes in priorities and cultivation of the other competencies through which geeks deliver value-added.

Competency 3: Ability to Juggle Multiple Tasks Simultaneously

Not all geeks can juggle balls, bowling pins, or chain saws, but the best geeks can juggle tasks. Participating in the give and take of complex technical business projects requires keeping track of and managing many facets of a project simultaneously. Although there are only so many hours in the day, geeks have to keep all the tasks in the air without letting any drop.

Effective juggling requires three basic skills:

- Keeping track of multiple active tasks
- Switching from one to the other with minimal time loss
- Setting priorities well

The number of active tasks a geek can track, the speed with which tasks are switched, and the importance of the tasks on which he chooses to work all contribute to a measurement of the geek's juggling skills.

Without strong juggling, it's nearly impossible to reach the highest levels of personal productivity. Very few technical project roles can be fulfilled by someone working in isolation on a single task. Imagine that you are a geek writing a project plan document, and your project manager runs into your office panicked about a customer who just called in with a problem. Telling her that you'll fix it as soon as you finish the document is unlikely to get you a reputation for responsiveness and cooperation.

Good juggling is also essential for expanding the number of competencies that can be applied simultaneously. Few of the competencies are exercised in isolation. They are all woven together into the fabric of the workday. The ability to juggle enables the application of the appropriate skill at the appropriate time. Juggling mediates the application of most of the other competencies.

Some people like to think that the ability to juggle is strictly inborn and can't be developed. I disagree. Juggling is not a simple thing that one either can or can't do. It's a talent that can be developed through practice. Like a bodybuilder who slowly adds weight to develop muscle, a task juggler can slowly add more tasks and track the changes in his or her abilities. With persistence and time, capacity grows.

Competency 4: Ability to Describe the Business Context of Technical Work

Because most geeks start their careers with extensive technical, and not business, training, they may have only a shallow understanding of the business context of their work. Through education and experience in the field, they develop a sense of a business context in which these technologies and processes exist. As professionals mature, they develop an increasing awareness of and ability to articulate the economic, political, and sociological context of technical work.

Professionals demonstrate this competency at many levels:

Low level: Faint awareness that there is a business context but not clear what it means or why it's important.

Medium level: More detailed awareness. They are aware of particular business goals associated with a project, what the goals are, how the project will meet the goals, and their own part in advancing the goals.

High level: More complete awareness. In addition to the competencies listed for the low and medium levels, geeks understand overall organizational strategy, how the project fits in, the political context, and the perspective of various stakeholders.

Very high level: Complete awareness. Geeks also understand such important concepts as industry dynamics, the current situation with competitors, and regulatory impacts.

The ability to perceive and describe the business context of technical work provides the foundation for more advanced competencies. Most geeks are frustrated that the language of business is business, not technology. A truly proficient geek understands and appreciates that business does not occur in the context of technology but technology is built and applied in the context of business. Inexperienced geeks tend to have the equation completely backward, believing that the business exists to support their precious technology.

What all of this boils down to is the ability to speak the language of business. I frequently hear clients complain that a geek is "too technical." In these cases, the client is rarely complaining that this person has too much technical breadth and depth. What the client is really complaining about is the geek's inability to understand or articulate the business context of the technical work. Although no geek is ever too strong technically, geeks are often deficient when it comes to speaking the language of business.

Competency 5: Ability to Forge Compromises Between Business and Technical Constraints

The big payoff for an organization comes when a professional can help forge the necessary compromise between business and technical constraints during the planning and execution of projects. Consider this scenario. John is a middle-level manager of software development for a midsized manufacturing company. The CEO of the firm has assembled a committee of business managers from across the company with the mission to "put the company on the Web." John has been invited to the first meeting to discuss the project.

The committee has already met a couple of times, and the chair kicks off the meeting. "John, we've decided that we want to build a knowledge warehouse and make it available on the intranet. What's it going to take to get this done?" Here, Sharon, the CFO, says, "My brother-in-law works for KNOW-IT-ALL.com, and we should use their software as a base." There is complete silence in the room.

Now John is faced with several issues and options. Does he just assume that the committee really knows what it wants? Do they understand the implications of what they're asking for? Do all the members of this committee really agree that they should use KNOW-IT-ALL.com? John has two basic directions in which to go.

First, he could ask more detailed questions about what the committee wants in the system, such as, "What data do you want in the system? What security should we be putting on the data? When do you need it? How much budget have you allocated?" This is the direction that I call "being a code vending machine." The technologist takes orders, machine-like, and produces the requisite code.

In the second, and more sophisticated, response, John asks, "Why do you want this? How do you envision this improving the business?" This would be the beginning of a partnership between John and the other members of the committee in which a productive and probably difficult conversation would begin. During that conversation, options, implications, costs, and benefits would be explored and evaluated, and important (and, often, difficult) compromises reached.

If John is able to drive a conversation within the organization about the business value of technology and to help his peers forge consensus on the business and technology strategy, he will have performed a tremendous service to the organization. Building a common vision among a management team is very difficult, but is also of very high value.

Forging compromises between technology and business interests is where advanced geekwork begins. Delivering this type of value requires a broad range of skills, including facilitation and influencing, as well as technical and business knowledge. Mastering this competency enables a geek to truly partner with business executives rather than being a mere servant.

Competency 6: Ability to Manage Client Relationships

Every geek has at least one client. Whether the client works for the geek's own company (for example, the CEO or CFO) or an outside organization is really not that important. The relationships with the leaders of the business must be actively cultivated and managed.

Managing client relationships is more complicated than it may seem and tougher than ordinary business relationships because it frequently means bridging the techie-nontechie gap. Furthermore, the traditional model of client relationship management—the one involving hearty handshakes, power suits, backslapping, prolonged lunches, and an occasional round of golf—is not just useless in this context, but presents an uncomfortable image for most geeks, because it involves personal relationships that do not conform to the problem-solution model of work.

Geeks also tend to view these relationships as one-sided and coercive. They think that managing a relationship is really about manipulating clients. It is the role of the manager to show geeks that managing client relationships is not about manipulation or other ethically dubious activities, but about helping clients to discover their own issues and showing them the way toward appropriate solutions to their problems using skills that include listening, appreciation for the business context of a solution, consensus building, and managing expectations. None of these skills tends to come naturally to geeks any more than small talk and golfing do. Nevertheless, they are skills that every ambitious geek must master—and it is your job, as manager, to show the way.

Competency 7: Ability to Manage Technical Teams

Very few truly important technical or business problems can be solved through the efforts of just one person. That means that most geekwork takes place in a team environment, a reality that provides both challenges and opportunities for individual geeks.

The challenge is that working in teams can be very difficult and significantly less productive than working alone. The "overhead" required for coordinating work and communication among several team members is significant. The benefit, however, is the opportunity is to expand one's value beyond the limits of personal productivity. To do so, however, a geek must learn to exercise leverage, the ability to use one's own skills to make others more productive.

Leverage can be measured fairly simply by increases (or, in some unfortunate cases, decreases) in group productivity. Assume that Sally alone can produce 3 widgets per day and each junior person in her department makes 2. Let's also assume that through her supervision, coaching, and training, the junior people under her care can increase their productivity to 2.5 widgets per day. Then if she supervises 12 junior people, the total output of her department has grown from 24 (12 × 2) to 30 (12 × 2.5) just based on her influence. She has improved their total productivity by 6 widgets per day. Even if she does nothing but supervise junior people and produces nothing herself, the value that she delivers is twice what she could produce alone.

Managing technical teams is one of the most common ways to leverage skills. It's important to note that there are many geeks who are neither interested in management nor temperamentally suited to it. It is not the kiss of death to their careers; there are other ways to continue building value. Some of the later competencies in this list speak to the alternatives.

For those who choose to follow the management path, overseeing a technical team is usually the first step in becoming a manager. Commonly, the first experience managing a team is also quite stressful. Managing a team of IT professionals is not a natural extension of being one.

Poor choice of a project manager is another common source of project failure. It is commonly assumed that the most talented technician should be appointed to manage a team of technicians. Nothing could be further from the truth. The skills of a good manager and those of a good technician are very different. Think carefully before assigning your best geek to lead other geeks.

Do not underestimate the complexity of managing even a small technical team. It is at least a part-time job, and could easily be more than a full-time job. Moreover, a poorly chosen manager can result in team productivity losses—as well as decreased employee morale and other unwanted consequences—if all of the elements for a successful team aren't in place.

Competency 8: Ability to Play Positive Politics

Geeks despise politics, yet they generally don't really understand what politics is about. In fact, it's not just geeks who have lost sight of the nature and role of politics. We live in an age of profound cynicism in which politics has taken on a very negative connotation. I see politics differently—and more positively. To me, it is the *process by which a group of people makes a decision*.

Over the course of my career, I've worked in several organizations where the senior managers claimed that there was no politics in the company. I always found this claim to be quite amusing, because, of course, there was politics. Every group of people has politics. Whenever there are two or more people, there is politics. If a group of people needs to make a decision, politics is involved.

The negative impression many people, including geeks, have of politics may result from thinking only about a subset of politics that I call self-interested politics. Most people find this subset quite disturbing. When people sense that the basis on which group decisions are being made changes from what's right for the organization to what's best for one individual, they get upset and cynical. Self-interested politics occurs when people try to force groups to make decisions that benefit them rather than the group as a whole.

Few people, on the other hand, think about Gandhi or Martin Luther King Jr. as politicians. They are remembered as leaders, but their leadership roles were profoundly political. In the microcosm of business, there are many revered managers within organizations who are thought of as influential in a very positive sense. They are not considered political creatures, yet their influence is exercised politically, in the sense that as they guide the decisions that direct an organization, they are taking part in a political process. If a participant in a political process advocates a position based on what best benefits the organization rather than what best benefits the participant, that is playing positive politics.

Positive politics is focused on understanding and balancing the goals of all the groups in the organization. As long as the focus of the exchange remains positive, it is useful to have a technological point of view represented in the determination of what is best for the organization.

It's very important for geeks to be able to play positive politics. If they don't, they will be shut out of the decision-making processes for their organization—and their input is critical to both their own success and the organization's. They have important information, ideas, and perspectives that need to be advocated.

Generally, geeks really want to play positive politics. They really want to have an effect on the direction of their organizations. Unfortunately, because of the combination of geek characteristics from Chapter Two (self-expression = communication, my facts are your facts, judgment is swift and merciless, and the problem-solution mind-set), they tend to be very hamfisted at participating in the political process. You must help them learn to get their valuable points across without alienating others in the process.

Competency 9: Ability to Help Expand Client Relationships

In this competency, we again tread on uncomfortable ground for most geeks. Many see themselves as people of ideas, not of commerce, and above the crass commercialism of the marketplace. This notion might be useful in a research laboratory, but it's not particularly useful in business. Whether an employee or contractor, deepening the engagement of one's organization with the business unit of the client is usually a primary goal.

It need not be a crass activity. Pursuing opportunities that are at odds with the interests of the client is not only crass but also unethical. Providing a service that benefits both the geek's organization and the client's is not. It is important for geeks to appreciate the difference.

This competency, as with most of the other advanced ones, relies heavily on the development of the more basic ones. Expanding the engagement with a client requires self-awareness, intelligence, honesty, perceptivity, and knowledge of one's own organization and negotiation skills.

Expanding a client relationship presumes that such a relationship is already in place and that it is being competently managed. If trust is lacking in the relationship, no amount of work will be sufficient to expand the engagement unless political forces, coercion, or extreme switching costs are involved. Let's take a brief look at each of the capacities that must be present:

1. *Identifying client needs.* In the course of normal work with a client organization, actively identifying client needs is the minimum skill required. It is harder to do than it sounds, because often clients don't have any idea what they want or need. A geek must therefore develop critical listening skills to understand what sorts of problems exist within the business organization.

2. *Crafting a solution.* Once a need has been identified, an appropriate solution must be crafted. Make no mistake: this also requires a high degree of skill. It combines technical breadth and depth, the ability to describe the business context of technical work, and the ability to forge compromises between business and technical constraints.

3. *Providing organizational introspection.* It is not enough to see both a problem and a solution clearly. It's necessary to understand honestly the capabilities of one's own organization, including its technical and managerial strengths and weaknesses. A professional must be both willing and able to raise hard questions about which parts of the solution can reasonably be provided and which must be sought elsewhere. This is where greed and ambition tempt wisdom.

4. *Matching needs and capabilities.* Once those questions are answered, the solution and the organizational capabilities must be appropriately matched to offer a comprehensive solution to the client.

5. *Building consensus.* At the same time, a professional must build consensus within the client organization around the nature of the problem and the appropriateness of the solution. This requires the ability to play positive politics.

Successfully completing all these steps isn't easy. It's a skill that few true geeks understand and even fewer possess, yet it is vitally important to integrating technology into the business enterprise. Without the ability to move beyond the simple technology service organization and the vending machine model, businesses will not realize the potential of automation. Expanding the client relationship allows the technology and business organizations to become partners for the betterment of the business.

Competency 10: Ability to Work Through Others, to Make Others Productive

This is another competency that enables geeks to exceed the limits of personal productivity. More specifically, it allows those who may not be interested or competent in management to leverage their personal talents and skills within the organization.

Management is not the only way to leverage one's talents. Some help others through providing technical leadership, assisting them with sticky technical problems, or teaching them ways to speed up their work. Others leverage through behavioral leadership. Many projects are very contentious and require someone to play psychologist, keeping everyone else productive and pulling in the same direction.

Although it is very difficult to measure the productivity of geekwork, clearly some people are better than others at making those around them more productive. Think about the people with whom you have worked on past projects. For most of us, there was one person who always seemed to make a difference on their project. When that person showed up, things started going right. That's a productivity booster. Then there are others who had the opposite effect—dooming even well-thought-out projects to failure and frustration. I call that group productivity busters.

As a young manager, one of my first challenges was to learn to identify the difference between productivity boosters and productivity busters. At one point, I was managing a group of around seventy-five people and had the good fortune to have two people among them who were absolutely technical gods. Technical gods are those geekiest of geeks whom all other geeks acknowledge as having superior technical skills. I could throw either John or Bob into anything. It didn't matter how complex the project, how intricate the technology, or how big a disaster the situation was. Within a day or two, they could figure out what was wrong with the technical design, the coding approach, or the project process.

So John and Bob became the go-to guys. Whenever a project seemed to be in trouble, I'd send one of them in. They were both equally capable technically, and neither had a managerial bone in his body. But over time, differences in their effectiveness became very apparent.

When John showed up, he would dive into the documentation, look at the code, check the tests, and diagnose the project. I'd usually show up a day or two later for a status meeting to see how things were going. When I arrived, there was always some sort of anti-enthusiasm cloud hovering in the room. Yes, progress was being made. Everyone understood what had gone wrong with the project and what had to be done to fix it, but no one seemed very excited, engaged, or energetic.

Bob worked essentially the same way as John, but there was an important difference: when I showed up after a couple of days, the project office would be a beehive of activity. People seemed focused, engaged, and enthusiastic. They all knew what had gone wrong with the project and understood what they were doing to fix it.

Wherever Bob went, the project team and the project got fixed. When John showed up, things got worse. What was the difference? The quality of their technical analysis was nearly identical. But their approaches to interacting with other people were completely different, and that made all the difference. Bob would act as a coach. He would explain what went wrong and give them direction and encouragement. He would challenge them, but in a nurturing way. John would berate and belittle the team, effectively calling people stupid. Bob was very effective at leveraging his technical knowledge by making whole teams much more effective than he could have been alone.

Despite his technical smarts, John's impact on projects was ultimately negative. They were worse off than when he arrived. In the end, I had to fire him, while Bob continued to be promoted into the stratosphere.

Competency 11: Ability to Manage Ambiguity

All technical work involves a great deal of ambiguity. No matter how clear things may seem on the surface, the creation and application of technology is a process fraught with misunderstandings, mistakes, and unknowns. Even the best technology projects are confusing and chaotic. Ambiguity arises because (1) most technology projects are highly complex and fragile constructions, (2) most technology projects are works in progress, with earlier stages of work leading to changes in later stages, and (3) the involvement of human beings as planners, implementers, and users contributes to whim and uncertainty.

Geeks like to use the metaphor "flying a plane while learning how to fly a plane" to describe their work. It means that whenever you embark on a complex technological project, you don't know everything you need to know to get the job done. Even if you've built twenty intranets, the twenty-first will be different because the client will be different and so will the technologies and even the economy and overall status of the Internet. You learn in the process of doing. Many geeks wish, on completion of a project, that they could start all over with the benefit of their newly acquired knowledge—the result would be so much better! Unfortunately, that's not the way life, or business, works.

You can probably figure out why, to most geeks, ambiguity is the worst place to be. And yet, a productive geek must learn to accept and cope with the reality of ambiguity (and to help other geeks do the same), that is, develop a high tolerance for working with uncertainty and create bubbles of clarity within which to be productive.

Being effective requires developing skills in both methods and continually expanding the level of ambiguity one is able to master. At the small end, we need to be able to define our own tasks for the hours and days ahead. At the large end, we may have to chart a course for an entire organization over a period of years.

Competency 12: Ability to Manage Time Horizons

The final way that geeks add value is through their mastery of time. A very subtle and complex topic, time is the backdrop on which business, technology, and indeed all the rest of human existence plays out. Although we rarely think about it as more than a cruel taskmaster to be resisted, time is present in everything we do. Like a neutral-colored canvas behind a painting, it provides a texture to all that we would build on it. Whether planning a project, scheduling a meeting, designing a system, or borrowing money, time is there, being planned, measured, manipulated, or conceptualized.

Managing time horizons is not the same thing as personal time management. Although they are very important, the techniques of personal time management are incorporated in this list of competencies under the heading of personal productivity.

At its most basic, the ability to manage time horizons is demonstrated through planning for the future. Planning requires:

1. Identifying clear goals
2. Thinking through the steps required to change the situation into the one idealized in the goals
3. Assembling and sequencing those steps into a coherent plan

As geeks gain experience, they are able to handle greater and more complex goals, which typically take longer to complete.

In addition to planning, managing time horizons requires foreseeing future events. Looking out into the future requires insight into both the micro and macro environments, including the personal, technical, business, and political environments. Whether guessing what will be the dominant database company a few years hence, predicting that a key employee will deliver his work late, or prognosticating that there will be a national recession, anticipating the future is extremely valuable to technical organizations.

Merely anticipating events, however, does little to drive successful organizations. That foresight must be translated into actionable information through some form of risk management. Actively managing risks can take many forms (and will be discussed in Chapter Ten), but for now, just think of it as planning for something like an earthquake. Geeks capable of solid risk management have reached a modest level of this competency.

Truly mastering time requires the ability to manipulate time itself, or more accurately, the ability to bend one's own and others' perception of time. Some managers view time as a river, on which we are carried along helplessly in a single direction—a linear model. Others see it as a cycle in which events are endlessly repeated, like the seasons or a product cycle—a cyclical model. Some see it as a combination of the two, as if climbing a spiral staircase where there are both cycles and progress—a helical model.

Bending time to one's will requires the ability to reconceptualize time. Some people do this instinctively, but few recognize its significance. To do this requires three distinct phases:

1. Recognize which model of time is being applied in a particular situation.

2. Change your own conception of which one should apply in this case.

3. Influence others to adopt your new point of view.

This is not an easy task, but it can be of extraordinary value to the success of a project. This can apply to both technical and business situations.

Here is an example of how it's done. A client comes to a geek with a request for a large systems development project. Traditional project management techniques in software development conceptualize time in a linear fashion, like a river. (The waterfall method, a traditional project approach will be described in more detail in a later chapter.) So the client thinks about the project in a monolithic fashion. She assumes that there is only one way to approach the project and that it must all be done at once. Based on the complexity of the project and vagueness of the definition, this assumption often serves as a barrier to success.

The experienced geek, however, will immediately set about recalibrating the client's sense of time, since a different model of time would make project success more likely. Our geek would attempt to change the client's vision of time from the linear model to the spiral model, enabling her to view the project as a series of smaller projects. Each turn up the spiral staircase will bring the project closer to the ultimate goal. This approach will enable them to test assumptions and refine the product in small increments, each of which has a better chance of actually being completed successfully.

Ultimately, managing time horizons is a subtle activity that takes on many forms and occurs on many levels simultaneously. Although somewhat abstract, it is no more so than the rest of geekwork.

Summary

FUNDAMENTAL QUESTIONS
- How do geeks perform geekwork?
- What competencies are critical for geek productivity?
- How do geeks progress in their careers and expand their ability to add value to their organizations?

KEY IDEAS
- Geeks relate to their work in complex ways that differ from those with more concrete work.

- The value that geeks add to organizations exceeds the delivery of technology.

- Geeks often don't know exactly how they perform their work.

- The twelve competencies not only describe how geeks relate to geekwork but also provide an outline of a career path with increasingly sophisticated interactions between geeks and geekwork.

PART TWO

The Content of Geek Leadership

Part Two examines the question of what geek leaders do using the second of the two major models that organize this book: the Content of Geek Leadership (Figure 1). This model outlines the four key responsibilities of geek leaders—the things that they do on a day-to-day basis that energize geeks, enable productivity, and align geekwork with the needs of the organization:

- Nurture motivation
- Provide internal facilitation
- Furnish external representation
- Manage ambiguity

Let's briefly introduce each of the responsibilities outlined in the model.

Nurture Motivation

The first of the four responsibilities is to nurture motivation among geeks. Most leaders want to inspire their followers, to spur them to action. Geek leaders want to foster the energy, drive, and commitment that come with a motivated workforce. Leaders usually try to

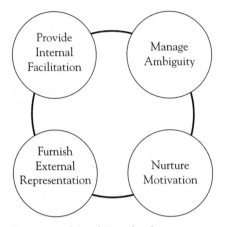

FIGURE 1. The Content of Geek Leadership.

use same motivational techniques with geeks that they do with other employees, but they rarely work and occasionally backfire. In many ways, it's easier to demotivate geeks than it is to motivate them.

In business, the most common approaches to motivation are incentives designed to elicit particular behavior, but geeks deliver value mostly through thought and not behavior, so conventional incentives don't work to spur creativity. In fact, leaders can't directly motivate geeks at all. Geek leaders mostly focus on creating the conditions under which motivation will develop. It's a bit like gardening. You can't make plants grow, but you can till the soil, fertilize, and water to try to create the conditions under which plants flourish. And just as each plant in a garden has its own special needs, the conditions that you try to create for motivation are special to the nature of geeks and geekwork.

Chapter Six explores how geek leaders create the conditions for motivation and identifies some common pitfalls that diminish motivation.

Provide Internal Facilitation

Typically, leaders are figures of authority who command the actions of followers with explicit instruction. But this sort of exercise of raw power is generally not productive in technical organizations; it can arouse the resistance of geeks and limit the quality and quantity of creative work that gets done.

Instead, geek leaders facilitate the flow of ideas and activities to ensure that teams and individuals within the group remain coordinated while working independently. In this way, leaders remain central to the activities of the organization without attempting to control them in the traditional hierarchical sense. In addition to coordinating tasks, geek leaders use their role to establish and maintain a work environment that is conducive to performing geekwork, designed to accommodate technological work and the human needs of geeks.

Chapter Seven describes how geek leaders provide internal facilitation.

Furnish External Representation

While providing supporting coordination inside the technology group, geek leaders also provide representation outside. In this capacity, leaders fill a number of critical needs related to the group's relationships with other areas within the organization, as well as with outsiders.

In many ways, the quality of external representation determines how successful technology groups become. For example, no matter how technically sophisticated and capable the geeks in a group are, if their geekwork is not properly aligned with the needs of the business, they will not deliver peak value. Alignment requires a well-managed relationship between the business units and the technology group.

Chapter Eight describes how geek leaders furnish external representation. It covers the functions of representations and also an overview of the various relationships in which geeks need to be represented.

Manage Ambiguity

The last, most important, and very subtle responsibility of a geek leader is managing ambiguity. Ambiguity, the absence of clarity, is inherent in all creative work, making progress difficult and elusive. Rather than being certain about what should be done and how to do it, geeks are usually uncertain about precisely what they are trying to accomplish and how they are going to go about it. It's not that they're confused; this is the nature of geekwork.

Chapter Nine discusses ambiguity and introduces a new model, the Hierarchy of Ambiguity, that describes the three types of ambiguity that geek leaders manage.

The Hierarchy of Ambiguity

Three categories of ambiguity must simultaneously be managed within technical organizations. Each level of ambiguity encompasses a range of questions about the workplace, its environment, and the work to be done. Together, they form the Hierarchy of Ambiguity (Figure 2), which has three levels:

- Environmental ambiguity
- Structural ambiguity
- Task ambiguity

Environmental Ambiguity

Environmental ambiguity encompasses questions about the big-picture issues surrounding any business organization, such as "Who are we?" "What does the outside world look like?" "How do we relate to the outside world?" "What is our purpose?" These are the

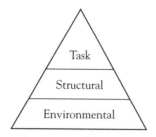

FIGURE 2. The Hierarchy of Ambiguity.

types of questions one answers in evaluating the high-level elements of the context of geek leadership.

The answers to these types of questions are for more than satisfying curiosity. In resolving these issues, leaders build the conceptual and emotional foundations on which technology organizations operate. These fundamental ideas serve to support all the responsibilities of the content of geek leadership.

Chapter Nine explores issues related to the management of environmental ambiguity.

Structural Ambiguity

Structural ambiguity encompasses issues related to the selection and organization of geekwork. Using information from the management of environmental ambiguity, leaders drive the selection and organization of work. These are questions related to projects and processes.

There are many ways to organize work, but projects are the most valuable form for geekwork. The nature of geekwork, the character of geeks, and the features of projects combine to make it the most potent form of organizational structure for technical work, conferring many benefits on the organizations that can use them.

Once organized into projects, geekwork must be structured around a process that provides a suitable approach to resolving the problems identified by projects.

Chapter Ten looks at managing structural ambiguity and examines projects and processes.

Task Ambiguity

The most detailed level of ambiguity in the hierarchy is task ambiguity. It encompasses issues related to the specifics of uniting geeks and geekwork. As structural ambiguity relates to selection and organizational strategies, task ambiguity relates to questions about the details of individual roles and tasks. The three main categories of task ambiguity are project roles, assignments, and judgments.

Project roles help define the task distribution and the social structure of work teams. They set expectations for goals, tasks, interactions, and behaviors that both guide and comfort geeks. A successful project must be structured correctly if it is to be successful.

Once project roles have been defined, geek leaders assign individuals to fill the roles. Although this may seem like a simple administrative duty, doing it well is quite subtle and also affects almost every facet of technology groups.

Finally, geek leaders help resolve task ambiguity by making judgments about product, process, and behavior. Although technology groups should be as self-regulating as possible, there are times when a leader must step in to ensure that proper standards are being applied.

Chapter Eleven describes the process of managing task ambiguity.

6

Nurturing Motivation

At some level, all leaders aspire to inspire. Everyone wants a motivated group: they're fun to be around, productive, and validating. If a leader has a motivated group, that must prove that she is a good leader, right? In fact, most business leaders are so desperate for staff with motivation that an entire industry has grown up around selling the abstract commodity of motivation. Platform speakers pack stadiums to extol its virtues. Rafts of posters display inspirational images. Libraries of books offer sappy parables. Lifetimes of commuter tapes and CDs drone on and on and on. Ironically, the seemingly endless supply of motivational material testifies to its futility. The industry attempts to fill a bottomless pit of apathy that stubbornly refuses to be filled. At the same time, the proliferation of these products speaks to the importance of the issue.

Even if you find this characterization of the value of motivational products harsh, different people respond differently to these generic messages. Each of the takes on motivation must resonate with some group of people, or it wouldn't survive in the Darwinian marketplace. But few, if any, of the well-worn messages resonate with geeks.

Imagine taking a group of geeks to a motivational sales meeting. The speaker at the front of the room engages the three hundred highly paid, extroverted, and successful salespeople in the room in a call-and-response on competition, challenge, success, and winning. The crowd is up on its feet, having a great time enjoying the company of comrades and competitors and reviewing ideas about how to go out and sell. There is electricity in the room, and you know that the glow will endure after they leave.

But the geeks you brought aren't on their feet. They aren't screaming back to the speaker. At first, they sit in the back, pondering the scene, mesmerized. Then someone starts sniggering and giggling. Eyes start to roll, and the judgment is in. They can't believe that this is even happening, that anyone is taken in by such vacuous content, and they're appalled that the objects of their disdain probably make more money than they do.

From what you already know about the cynical and independent nature of geeks it shouldn't be surprising that they wouldn't respond to this sort of message or presentation style. Geeks are just not rah-rah people.

The first of the four responsibilities of the geek leader is nurturing motivation. It can't be done in the traditional manner. You've got to help geek groups get motivated in a way that's compatible with their personalities and the constraints of geekwork.

Can You Motivate Geeks?

One of the major failings of the motivation industry is its failure to account for differences in those who would be motivated. Most of what's being peddled is designed as a one-size-fits-all approach, as if all people are exactly alike. What little targeted material exists focuses mostly on salespeople, so when you're trying to motivate geeks, you're pretty much on your own.

Clearly, geeks *can* be motivated. Engaged, enthusiastic teams turn out exciting products all the time. New software hits the streets every day. Web sites are updated regularly. Although the general project success rate in the IT industry is rather dismal, products do ship, and it's usually a motivated team that manages to beat the odds and complete a project successfully.

So the difficult question to answer is not whether geeks can be motivated, but whether there is anything you as a leader can do to motivate a team engaged in geekwork. What actions can you take? What statements can you make? Is there anything you can do to win over their hearts and minds?

The answer is yes . . . and no. Although it is difficult to motivate someone to contribute to a creative effort like geekwork, it is very easy to demotivate them. There are significant barriers to motivating geeks, but you can create the conditions under which motivation can thrive.

To make sense of this we must first take a closer look at nature of motivation itself and its sources.

Sources of Motivation

For millennia, people have recognized the centrality of motivation to the human experience and have attempted to explain its presence or absence in individuals or groups. Nevertheless, this complex phenomenon remains illusive, even now resisting comprehensive explanation. Various theories attribute levels of motivation to one or more of the following:

- Biological imperatives—the drives for food, shelter, and reproduction
- Personality—the patterns of behavioral dispositions that remain relatively static within each person over time
- High-level cognitive needs such as self-expression and fulfillment
- Social environmental factors

If nothing else, this list helps clarify the difficulty of motivating others in the workplace (or anywhere else, for that matter). Leaders have limited influence over most of these factors that are theorized to affect motivation, reminding us that it is an internal emotional state not easily touched by others.

When looking at the workplace, psychologists have found it useful to categorize a person's motivation to perform a specific task as one of two distinct types: intrinsic or extrinsic. According to

Harvard Business School professor Teresa Amabile, a pioneer in the research of motivation for creativity, "People are *intrinsically motivated* when they seek enjoyment, interest, satisfaction of curiosity, self-expression, or personal challenge in work. People are *extrinsically motivated* when they engage in the work in order to obtain some goal that is apart from the work itself." [1]

An intrinsically motivated person engages in a task based purely on factors internal to the person, the task, and the person's feelings about the work and reasons for doing it. It may be that it's interesting, challenging, or exciting, or it may be that the person is engaging in it for self-expression or personal growth. The factors affecting intrinsic motivation are completely contained within the work and the person doing the work. No outside incentives are involved.

An extrinsically motivated person engages in a task to achieve something beyond the work. Extrinsic motivators originate outside the work but may be tied to it (examples are incentives, rewards, recognition, and deadlines). Bonus programs are the classic example of an extrinsic motivator. One does the work not because of the rewards of the work but for the rewards the work may bring—the big payoff.

Most people find that motivation for a particular task is formed by a combination of intrinsic and extrinsic factors, creating a complex of reasons that provide the drive to engage in and complete a particular task. For example, you might assign Sally to a project that she is particularly interested in, that provides the opportunity to learn about a new technology that she has not been exposed to. Her intrinsic motivation to do a good job on the project would be rather high. When you offer her the assignment, she's probably not going to ask how it will affect her annual bonus. She just wants to dig into the fascinating material. But no matter how interesting or exciting the project may be, Sally's probably not going to be too excited about writing weekly status reports. There's no intrinsic motivation for that, only compliance with policy and rules, an extrinsic motivator.

As a manager, you have more control over extrinsic motivators than intrinsic ones. You can try to create the conditions under which intrinsic motivation occurs, but you have rather limited direct control over those factors. However, you do have significant control over incentives such as contingency payments, recognition, and rewards. Many managers confuse manipulating extrinsic motivational factors with being a motivational leader. They are quite different. Providing incentives alone is not leadership. It is bribery.

Motivating Geeks

Which matters more when trying to motivate geeks: intrinsic or extrinsic factors? Which should you as a leader focus on developing? And how can you do it? To answer these questions, it's important to recognize the unique nature of geeks and geekwork and to accommodate it when developing your strategy for motivation.

Most geekwork is essentially creative problem solving, so when you consider how to motivate geeks, it's important to examine the effect of different types of motivators on the impulse toward creativity and productivity.

Traditional management approaches focus almost exclusively on providing extrinsic motivators, assuming that incentives properly aligned with organizational or project goals will always elicit desired behaviors from employees. If you clearly identify a goal and provide an explicit incentive (money, time off, promotion, or recognition, for example), then employees will do what you want them to do.

Unfortunately with geekwork, you're trying to do more than elicit behavior; you want to encourage creativity. Can extrinsic motivators alone engage the focused mental energy of a group of geeks? No. Amabile has found that most creativity springs from intrinsic motives. Intellectual and emotional engagement with a problem breeds creative problem solving, not externally defined enticements. Incentives cannot create engagement. True engagement with a problem must come from within.

Extrinsic motivators may have helpful, detrimental, or inconsequential effects on creativity depending on how they are structured. If a geek is uninterested in a problem, even massive incentives, such as potentially high-value stock options, cannot make the problem interesting. Even if the geek agrees to work on an uninteresting problem with only the hope of attaining a grand reward, don't expect stellar work. If instead he is initially interested in working on a problem, some extrinsic motivators may intensify commitment, while others may diminish engagement by drawing attention away from the problem and onto the incentive itself. Providing extrinsic incentives alone is insufficient for building a high-performance creative team.

But what can you as a leader do to create intrinsic motivation? Nothing directly. You can't create intrinsic motivation, but you *can* create the environmental conditions under which it develops, just as you can provide conditions under which it is killed. *Your challenge is to encourage intrinsic motivation and support it with appropriate extrinsic motivation.*

To create the environment in which creativity and energy thrive, you should:

- Select wisely
- Manage meaning
- Communicate significance
- Show a career path
- Projectize
- Encourage isolation
- Engender external competition
- Design interdependence
- Limit group size
- Control resource availability
- Offer free food . . . intermittently

Select Wisely

The most important thing you as a leader can do to encourage intrinsic motivation is to choose the right people to be on the right projects. It may seem obvious, but the most effective way to help a team build intrinsic motivation is to pick people who want to be on the team in the first place. Since you can't imbue geeks with internally generated enthusiasm, select for it. There are many other factors that must be considered, but initial interest in the technology, the business, or a role on a project should be one of the primary considerations when making assignments.

Chapter Eleven covers additional factors to consider in properly balancing the skills of team members.

Manage Meaning

The second most important thing that a leader can do to support the development of intrinsic motivation is to frame reality, to actively manage meaning in the workplace. In their frustratingly ambiguous world of questions, assumptions, and provisional facts, geeks constantly need to make sense of their environment and the meaning of their work. They need some fixed point in the distance to help guide day-to-day decisions and provide a coherent context to the nearly endless stream of confusion.

Without some sense of the larger meaning of their work, it becomes nearly impossible to generate consistent intrinsic motivation to slog through the implementation of a complex solution to a complicated problem. Although the nature of the problem may be compelling at the outset, no project provides uninterrupted interest. Pushing through the tedious and frustrating parts requires some sense that it's worth the trouble.

That's where you as a leader come in. You must deliver the meaning of all the disparate facts, framing the situation and defining reality. If you don't take explicit control of the meaning of situations, they will either remain ambiguous or be defined by others. In the absence of clarity, rumor and innuendo often take over. A group of smart geeks can develop some wild theories about why no one is telling them what's going on, and, trust me, most of those creative ideas are not productive.

Geeks develop a sense that their work has meaning by viewing their individual work through the lens of their personal values. If work fulfills their most important personal values, then it has meaning. If it does not, then it has considerably less meaning. In order to make this evaluation, they need to be able to view their work in its broadest context, making sense of how it relates to others' work, the organization as a whole, and even society in general. Without the ability to understand the context of work, it's very hard to evaluate its connection to personal values.

For geeks, I've observed that the most commonly held values are these:

- Developing knowledge
- Creating intricate and beautiful systems
- Proving potential
- Making money
- Helping others
- Enhancing career growth

Communicate Significance

Although the meaning of a situation provides the context for geek-work, it doesn't necessarily convey the importance or urgency of a project. The frame provided by meaning may or may not indicate the importance with which leadership regards the work.

Too often, a leader will explain what role a new technology plays in a business and assume that everyone naturally shares the same understanding of its significance. It's vital to be explicit since some will misunderstand the centrality of their work, and others may develop delusions of grandeur. Clearly, it's much easier to develop intrinsic motivation for significant work than marginal or irrelevant work.

Show a Career Path

Given the ambiguity of geekwork and the complexity of how geeks perform it, one's career path can often be difficult to understand.

Geeks are exposed to two primary messages about career progress, both of them misleading: you can further your career by building technical skills or by acquiring power, that is, by becoming a manager. Many geeks have a vague sense that there's more to advancing their careers than just acquiring new technical knowledge, but they often don't know what it is. So they assume that the business cultural focus on management must be the right way, no matter how disinterested in management or temperamentally unsuited they may be.

Most geeks are motivated to advance in their careers, but have little information about how to do it. If you can help them see how to grow, to enhance the value they deliver in ways that are compatible with individual interests and skills, and then link that to current work, geeks will often develop intrinsic motivation for the work.

You can use the twelve competencies outlined in Chapter Five as a guide to help decide potential career paths for geeks.

Projectize

One of the simple things that most of the motivational gurus get right is goal setting. They extol the virtue of setting explicit goals to focus attention and energies on specific, measurable, and achievable targets. In geekwork, the best way to set a goal is to define a project to address it.

The alternative, working on an endless treadmill where one day is the same as the next, and without any measurable achievements, is not engaging. Projects help turn work into a game, and geeks love games with objectives that delineate goals and success criteria.

Chapter Ten will discusses projectizing in more detail.

Encourage Isolation

In the age of ubiquitous communication and cross-functional teams, it seems a bit ironic that isolated groups have an easier time developing intrinsic motivation than do more interconnected ones.

Although geeks need free-flowing communication within their own work groups, collective seclusion provides fertile soil for motivation, cultivating cohesion, and concentration. For example, when Steve Jobs wanted to focus and motivate the original Macintosh development team at Apple Computer, he moved the group to an entirely different building to isolate them.

Physical isolation works in several ways to enhance motivation. Isolation from other parts of the organization provides an opportunity to focus on the geekwork at hand without the distractions of other projects or office gossip. Given that individuals vary widely in their ability to concentrate in the presence of common workplace diversions, distance balances the group by limiting access to those distractions. Uneven concentration can reduce productivity and sap motivation.

In addition, remoteness offers the opportunity to develop group cohesion and identity that imparts a sense of distinctiveness and pride, enhancing intrinsic motivation. Groups are more strongly inspired when they feel that their work is important and they are part of a privileged elite to take on such vital work.

Finally, removing the group from the local political environment can help create intrinsic motivation. Geeks are typically not politically savvy and find engaging in the push and pull of politics both distracting and demoralizing. They want to feel that everyone is behind their efforts. The natural jockeying of decision making may leave them feeling otherwise.

Isolation can be counterproductive if the group is completely disconnected from the rest of the organization. Not only can their work diverge from the needs of the organization, but they can lose the sense of importance without consistent communication and reinforcement. You need to make sure that someone within the project team plays the role of advocate for and interface to the rest of the organization to maintain productive links without sacrificing isolation.

Encouraging isolation is especially difficult when using virtual teams spread across time zones, office complexes, and even international boundaries. Individual isolation works against the creation of group identity, interdependence, and elitism, challenging group creativity and motivation.

Engender External Competition

Geeks love a good fight—not the fisticuff variety, but a good contest. It brings out their macho competitive spirit and love of games, allowing them to engage their seldom-expressed enthusiasm. Most of the highly motivated and productive groups that I've encountered have found meaning in battling some form of bogeyman. The joy of creation is considerably enhanced by the thrill of participating in the defeat of evil with ingenuity. A good competition also helps to develop group cohesion. Nothing is so unifying as the presence of a common enemy. Intragroup rivalries are set aside, and power struggles are subordinated to the common goal of winning the competition.

Just make sure that the competition does not set up destructive internal rivalries between different units within the same organization. This can lead to long-term animosities, wasted emotion, and duplicated efforts. Occasionally, it is possible to create temporary competition, but make sure that it takes on more of the character of a foot race than a war.

Design Interdependence

An old cliché says that in battlefield foxholes, soldiers don't fight for their country, they fight for each other. Fear and self-preservation pale when confronted with the needs of others. So deeply rooted are psychological bonds of human pack animals that even now, many of our most cherished stories express the nobility and heroism of self-sacrifice for the benefit of comrades.

This primal drive to fulfill the needs of others is present on the frontlines of geekwork too. This powerful narrative is much more than a curiosity of rare circumstances. It plays itself out daily in all of our self-constructed, heroic, Walter Mittyesque narratives that comprise our lives.

The personal bonds of loyalty that develop between peers are often more important in developing intrinsic motivation than are those between a geek and a leader. When a colleague is relying on you to complete your work, it's much easier to put in the extra effort for that person than it is just to meet some externally imposed deadline.

Limit Group Size

The larger the work group is, the less conducive is the environment for developing intrinsic motivation. As group size grows, colleagues become less individuals and more an undistinguished mass of anonymous faces. If a geek feels like a cog in a giant machine, the pull of interdependence weakens substantially.

In fact, at some point, a group can grow so large that it discourages motivation. I think of it as being like the income tax effect. Many people who consider themselves to be honest and upstanding citizens, people who would never think of picking someone's pocket, are perfectly comfortable lying about their income on their tax returns. They don't feel that they're doing anything dishonest since they can't see or identify with the victim. The fact that the victim is some distant monolith somehow absolves them of the sin. Large, abstract groups don't elicit the same feelings of obligation or loyalty.

Control Resource Availability

Another way to encourage intrinsic motivation is to carefully control the resources available to a project team, whether money, people, time, or training. There's a delicate balance of resources that will encourage a group's enthusiasm. Too many resources or too few can diminish interest in the work.

Limiting resources too tightly can cause significant problems. If a team believes that deadlines are tight, that's fine, but if they feel that they are impossible, they will not commit to meeting them and won't really try. If a group lacks necessary technical skills to complete a project but is denied training, they will withdraw and try to learn while ignoring schedules.

More counterintuitively, lavishing a team with resources can also diminish engagement too. Limitations of time and budget force a group to think carefully about a problem and to forge a creative solution that meets as many of the constraints as possible. With too many resources, there's no challenge. Geeks find no joy in overly simplistic puzzles.

You've got to strike the balance by gauging what resources are absolutely necessary and which constitute luxuries.

Occasionally, it's okay to make seemingly unreasonable demands of a group. It focuses their creativity and challenges them to deliver, creating a sense of excitement. Just don't do it too often if you don't want every time estimate padded and every budget bloated.

Offer Free Food . . . Intermittently

Never underestimate the power of free food. I can't offer any rational explanation, but for geeks, even those making sizable incomes, free food offers major support to motivation development—far more than an equivalent amount of cash. It may be due to the long hours or to some primitive instinct related to feeding together, but if you occasionally fill the office with free sodas, subsidized snacks, pizza, and beer, the productivity boost far exceeds the cost. However, if you always have free food around, it seems to lose its motivating value. Geeks start to view it as a fundamental human right rather than a motivational perk.

Demotivating Geeks

Unfortunately, in many ways, it's easier to sap the enthusiasm out of a group of geeks than it is to inspire them. I'm not suggesting that these are fragile groups that need to be treated with kid gloves. On the contrary. Intrinsic motivation, once developed, is quite resilient, but its initial formation can be tenuous. Unless the problem is so compelling, the technology so fascinating, or the meaning so deeply important that everyone on a project is instantly enthralled with participation, you've got to be careful about inadvertently demotivating a group.

Many things that managers commonly do damage intrinsic motivation by either diminishing the quality of the work environment or misusing extrinsic motivators. Maintaining an optimal environment for motivation for geeks requires careful thought, since some traditional motivational management techniques that work well for others do not here.

These are the common pitfalls:

- Exclusion from decision making
- Inconsistency
- Excessive monitoring
- Focus on tasks, not goals
- Unqualified evaluation
- Misaligned extrinsic motivators
- Artificial deadlines
- Changing deadlines
- Organizational disinterest
- Teams without skills

Exclusion from Decision Making

Geeks hate being left out of decision-making loops, receiving directives after all the discussions and deliberations are finished. In their technocentric worldview, it's inconceivable that good decisions could be made without their being consulted. But more than calling into question the value of the decisions, it also undermines their feelings of competence and independence, limiting their sense of control over their environment necessary to develop intrinsic motivation. Leaving them out also invites insecurities about the level of trust and esteem in which a leader holds geeks. Although not every decision can include everyone, using key geek representatives will be helpful, and in the absence of that, explanations of decisions can help alleviate problems.

Inconsistency

Geeks are equipped with exquisitely tuned hypocrisy detectors that sound an alarm whenever any sort of inconsistency or double standard may be present in a leader's behavior. The strength of belief in fairness and meritocracy combines with distrust of hierarchy to leave leaders in a bit of a sensitive spot. Every comment, every action is monitored for consistency and coherence and will be challenged if it fails to stand up to the test. Inconsistency undermines motivation by distracting from the engaging nature of the work. The more attention and emotional energy a geek invests in monitoring a leader's behavior, the less there is available for engagement with the work.

Once seen as inconsistent, a leader will have to struggle to regain confidence. Geeks tend to view inconsistent managers as either dumb or duplicitous, and sometimes both. Once categorized as either, it isn't easy to rebuild relationships. The only easy way out of this trap is to avoid it altogether.

Excessive Monitoring

Geeks expect their expertise to confer on them the benefits of professionalism equal to those of any lawyer or doctor, with one of the most cherished benefits being independence to determine one's own work pattern. Having someone look over their shoulder feels too much like being an apprentice. More important, it is taken as a sign of mistrust or lack of confidence. Naturally, managers feel that their job is to direct and monitor the work of their subordinates, which sets up a continual problem within technical organizations. One of the greatest insults a geek can hurl at a manager is "micromanager." The feeling of being mistrusted quickly subverts intrinsic motivation.

Focus on Tasks, Not Goals

Since a great deal of intrinsic motivation is drawn from the context, the meaning of a task, it shouldn't be surprising that when a leader gives direction only through specific task assignments, enthusiasm diminishes. Without any understanding of the goals for a task, geeks start to feel like technology vending machines, dispensing solutions on demand. Under these circumstances, they engage in the creative work task with the same excitement as a soft drink vending machine dispensing a drink. It may work, but don't expect anything more than you ask for, and you may not get anything at all.

Unqualified Evaluation

One of the great human dilemmas of all time, "Who is qualified to judge me?" plays out in its own small way in technical groups. Rather than being a moral question of righteousness, here it becomes a practical problem related to the unusual knowledge inversion, where subordinates know more about their work than their supervisors do. Most bad performance reviews that I have delivered over the years are followed by the "you don't understand what I do" conversation. Specialists feel that only other specialists are qualified to evaluate their work, and the fear of being unfairly criticized undermines commitment.

You need not surrender your responsibility to evaluate the work of those with specialized technical knowledge. The key is being very clear about both technical and nontechnical expectations of the job. Few geeks are ever given clearly articulated guidelines for the nontechnical components of their work, but if you look closely at Chapter Five on performing geekwork, you'll notice that only one of the twelve ways geeks add value relates directly to technology. Spell out complete expectations for both technical and nontechnical contributions, and geeks will not only better understand how to be successful in their jobs, but you'll be qualified to judge their performance.

Misaligned Extrinsic Motivators

One of the most common mistakes managers make is trying to use extrinsic motivators with geeks in the same ways that they use them for salespeople. Contests, commissions, plaques, and pens don't carry the same weight and often undermine interest in the task at hand by trivializing geeks' sense of meaning.

Reward systems that emphasize personal over group performance can impair group cohesion, limiting information flow and creativity. You can also end up in a situation where an overall project failed, but many individuals are considered successes. In extreme cases, individual awards or bonuses can pit geeks against each other in a zero-sum game that turns colleagues into competitors.

On the other end of the spectrum, some extrinsic motivators are tied to overall company goals over which individuals and even whole groups feel that they have no control. If geeks believe that they have no control over the measures of success, the incentives offer little motivation and can even demotivate.

Finally, even when properly aligned, some inducements can be of such magnitude (for example, stock options potentially worth millions of dollars) that their presence is a distraction from work and reduces intrinsic motivation. When you're too busy trying to decide which Caribbean island to buy for your retirement, the details of programming can seem petty and uninteresting.

Artificial Deadlines

Although deadlines are important for helping bring a project to completion, patently artificial deadlines can undermine motivation to meet them. Geeks hate it when someone picks a random date out of the air and expects them to work night and day to meet it, especially when they can see that nothing else in the organization will change if the deadline slips. Schedules are most effective when everyone involved in a project accepts it as both reasonable and necessary. Whereas good deadlines are a powerful motivational tool, artificial ones undermine commitment.

One of the most effective ways to make a deadline real to a group is to tie it to some sort of external event or commitment, such as an industry trade show, a product launch event, or a major holiday. Deadlines that are tied to immovable events are much more likely to be accepted as real than those that are seemingly selected with a dart and a calendar. The more public the failure to meet a delivery date will be, the more likely that it will be met.

Changing Deadlines

Little else confirms suspicious geeks' disbelief in random deadlines as much as the changing deadline. The more often a due date is changed, the less commitment any deadline will elicit. Not only does a group lose the opportunity to gain motivation from a credible date, the constantly shifting date itself becomes a distraction from the work.

Organizational Disinterest

If meaning is one of the primary stimulants of intrinsic motivation, then lack of meaning is one of its most significant barriers. Unless the work itself is completely engrossing, it's very hard for anyone to get excited about working on a project that has been deemed unimportant by either word or action. Although few leaders intend to communicate the unimportance of a project, it's very easy to give that impression through disengagement or omission.

Teams Without Skills

Feeling helpless or adrift diminishes motivation. Only Chicago Cubs fans seem excited by being associated with a perpetually losing team. An underdog with a chance is exciting; a guaranteed loser is not. When project teams are constructed without the requisite technical or management skills, the first to know are the geeks on the team, and if they feel helpless to acquire the necessary expertise, the work will receive little energy.

Summary

FUNDAMENTAL QUESTIONS

- How do geek leaders nurture motivation?
- How is nurturing motivation different from providing incentives?
- What is different about motivating geeks from motivating other employees?
- How do many traditional approaches to motivation demotivate geeks?

KEY IDEAS

- Most leaders attempt to motivate employees with incentives designed to elicit particular behavior, but because geeks don't deliver most of their value with behavior but through thought, these traditional incentives are often inappropriate.

- There are two distinct categories of sources for motivation to complete geekwork: extrinsic, where one is motivated to perform a task because of something beyond the task, and intrinsic, where one is motivated to perform a task because of something integral to the task itself. Intrinsic motivation is more important for productivity in completing geekwork.

- Leaders cannot force others to generate intrinsic motivation for creative thought, but they can create the conditions under which motivation flourishes. And they can create the conditions that are likely to kill intrinsic motivation.

7

Providing Internal Facilitation

Traditionally, hierarchical leaders and subordinates have well-defined roles prescribed by organizationally assigned power and authority. Leaders delegate tasks, power, and authority to their subordinates; monitor their execution; and retain centralized decision-making authority for any matters that have not been explicitly delegated. In addition, leaders are responsible for setting direction and coordinating activities between subordinates.

But in technology groups, this approach rarely works well. The traditional top-down approach to internal management breaks down because of the three key reasons for geek leadership. Geeks as a group do not respond well to the centralized authoritarian approach to management. They resist overt attempts to control them and do not respond to conventional incentives. The knowledge inversion of geekwork similarly works to undermine the hierarchical approach to management as well. Leaders who do not completely understand all the details of all their subordinates' work can't direct them effectively. And finally, the diminished importance of power as a means of control and behavior as a means of value delivery limits the success of the hierarchical approach.

So what do geek leaders do to create productive groups instead of conventional downward delegation? They provide internal facilitation, the second major responsibility of a geek leader. Internal facilitation covers two categories of activities and responsibilities of the geek leader: establishing and maintaining the local work environment and task coordination.

Facilitation Versus Control

Most conventional ideas about leadership are centered around the notion of power—the ability to influence the actions and behavior of others. But for geek leaders, power is of little use since productivity is grounded in thought, not behavior. And so the closely allied idea of control is similarly less useful to geek leaders than traditional leaders.

In some ways, control is an even less useful idea than power when working on technological projects. Control implies an absolute power, more than just influence over the behavior of others, but a nearly mechanistic ability to direct with absolutely no chance of resistance. To a geek, the word *control* conjures images of a remote control for a television or stereo. Being controlled is not something that geeks typically aspire to.

Facilitation is quite different. A leader who focuses on facilitating activities is more concerned with ensuring smooth information flow, recognizing and satisfying interdependencies, overcoming obstacles, and assisting each person to fulfill his or her individual goals. Facilitation does not require power, and so does not arouse the indignation of geeks. They welcome facilitation, whereas they resist control.

But don't think that a facilitator is powerless. In fact, by becoming a central locus for information critical to the success of each individual, a leader who focuses on facilitation has constant access to status information and influence over what internal communication takes place. By controlling both information flow and agenda, a leader develops considerable power without arousing the defenses of geeks. Ironically, a leader who grabs control too openly loses power to resistance.

The Challenge of Facilitation

For leaders used to thinking about their roles in terms of power and control, taking on a purely facilitative role can be difficult and emotionally trying. Managers used to working in a traditional hierarchical fashion often become comforted by the idea that they control the success of their organization. Of course, even in traditional organizations this feeling of control is substantially illusory. In fact, the higher anyone goes in an organizational structure, the more dependent that person becomes on subordinates for success. But the feeling of being in control becomes deeply ingrained in daily life and even in the internalized identity of a leader. So for a leader, taking on a facilitative rather than a controlling role can violate deeply held images of self, arousing surprisingly powerful negative emotional responses.

Another challenge for managers is that they often begin to associate control with status and believe that adopting a facilitative stance implies a diminution of personal status. As with pack animals, relinquishing status violates values deeply entrenched in our collective psyches and cannot easily be overlooked. Leaders harbor fears not only of losing control and status; they also fear that others will view it that way. So even if they believe that facilitating is not a loss of status, they still may be concerned that others might think so.

For geek leaders who start their careers in technical work, facilitation offers an additional challenge. Facilitation activities don't easily conform to the problem-solution model so common in the thinking of engineers. They are constantly looking for a systemic way to address the ongoing need for facilitation, trying to apply a mechanistic view of human groups that doesn't really apply to creative work. One can't "solve the problem" of facilitation. It's the sort of ongoing activity that geeks usually resist.

Establishing and Maintaining Local Work Environment

One of the primary responsibilities of leadership is to set the tone for the work environment. You may have little direct control over the productivity of geeks, but you do have the ability to encourage the development of an environment conducive to productive work. Although there's no magic formula for creating a perfect environment, when considering what sort of environment to establish it's important to think about the nature of geeks and of geekwork.

By force of habit, most leaders tend to reestablish work environments in which they have worked previously where they felt comfortable, repeating patterns from earlier in their career rather than considering the specific needs of a particular group of followers or their work. This is unfortunate since so many leaders are flexible enough to be comfortable in many different types of environments and are perfectly capable of creating one conducive to productive geekwork. It's not that they actively resist creating an environment in which geekwork can thrive, but that they simply make unexamined assumptions that all work environments should feel like.

But even for leaders who are sensitive to the needs of geeks and geekwork, it's not obvious what sort of environment to create or how to create it. Luckily, many different types of environments can be very effective for geeks. A few key characteristics must be observed in order to create a high-performance culture.

Creating Community and Culture

Two of the most important elements of establishing a productive environment are defining and creating community and culture. A group of geeks constitutes a community when they work together and feel a common bond of identity. A community shares a common purpose or idea that helps define the boundaries of the community as well as the internal roles and relationships. But a group that identifies itself as a community may or may not be productive or useful; it must also have a culture that supports productivity.

The culture of a community grows over time, slowly accumulating as individuals work together, share common challenges, establish patterns of interactions, and discover what works well for them and what doesn't. These patterns of interactions become embedded in the thinking of the individuals in the community as assumptions about how their group works. But if culture is built on the basis of shared experiences, how much control over the establishment of culture does a leader really have?

Because a leader is not involved in every group interaction, there are significant limitations on how much a leader can influence the development of culture. All too often, leaders like to think that giving lectures espousing particular values is the same as establishing culture, but clearly it's not. Assumptions grounded in shared experiences are much more influential in the thinking of group members than values from a lecture. In almost every geek group in which I've worked, the managers and leaders have taken great pains to talk about one aspect of the culture or another while the rest of the group rolls their eyes and laughs, knowing that the leader's behavior contradicts his espoused values. Over the years, I've run into any number of leaders who love to give lectures on the importance of customer service, but whenever they are faced with tough decisions, they opt to value budget or schedule over the customers' interest.

It's best to choose a few core values that you consider to be the most important to establish an appropriate environment for productivity and to focus on inculcating these values in the group. It can't be done with one speech or training seminar; it will permeate the culture only through repeated experience. Be sure that your actions and judgments continually support and reinforce these core values so that your actions don't undermine your words.

Whether you are taking over an existing group or establishing a new one, one of the first things you must consider is how to create community among geeks and what sort of community that should be. For existing groups, you must consider whether you want to try to change the culture and, if so, what aspects of it you want to try to change. In many ways, it's somewhat easier establishing new groups and laying a new foundation rather than remodeling an old one.

At their core, questions of community and culture are related to the leader's role in managing ambiguity, which will be discussed in more detail in Chapters Nine through Eleven. Both are approaches to dealing with the complex cacophony of information inherent in the geek workplace.

Creating Safety for Ideas

Perhaps the most important concept to build into the culture of a geek group is safety for ideas. Since geekwork is almost exclusively about harnessing the creativity and ideas of geeks, if people don't feel safe to express their best ideas, the quality and quantity of production will suffer. Generally, people feel very vulnerable revealing ideas for fear of rejection.

The feeling of safety must extend to two distinct levels: it must be safe to express ideas about the substance of the geekwork being produced and about the process by which the work takes place.

In order to create safety for ideas, everyone must believe that freedom of speech exists within the community. There can be no taboo subjects or heresies that cannot be expressed without fear of retribution. It must be safe to question not only the decisions of leaders and managers but their authority. Geeks must have no fear of retribution for whatever comments they make so long as they are made in the service of progress.

More than just creating an environment of the freedom to speak, everyone should believe that what they have to say is valuable and becomes part of the discussion about how to proceed. It must be clear that those who contribute insights and well-thought-out approaches to problems and obstacles are considered valuable, high-status members of the group and are rewarded accordingly.

This is not to say that every person in a group of two hundred must have a voice in every decision, but that within the confines of one's particular role, the group values that they express their most important ideas. And for things about which one feels passionately, it must also be safe to exceed the bounds of one's typical role from time to time and offer thoughts on issues beyond one's authority.

Finally, given the nature of creativity, it must also be safe to make stupid comments sometimes without being dismissed by the group as an idiot. People with the most creative minds often come up with many bad ideas before coming up with a great one, so everyone must clearly know that making a contribution that ultimately turns out to be laughable does not result in permanent branding as a moron.

Creating Forums for Conflict and Search for Truth

In traditional settings, ideas are generated and then vetted and decided on by the central hierarchical leader. The openness of the environment and the quality of decisions are entirely dependent on the talent and consistency of the leader.

Once you create an environment in which everyone feels safe to express ideas, it becomes important to develop a way to channel the cacophony into decisions that optimize the productivity of the group and the quality of its output. Allowing everyone to express opinions does not mean that a group will make good choices.

In geek organizations, an important goal is to harness decentralized creativity without creating the communications bottleneck or the bounded vision that comes with centralized leadership. You must develop a different approach to channeling, vetting, and debating ideas to ensure that the best ones get adopted.

In order to do this, leaders create forums into which these ideas flow, where geeks can collect and debate ideas on particular topics. To do this, individuals and groups are assigned and held accountable for decisions related to some aspect of the product or the process. These forums should be composed of groups of people who represent the critical interest groups of a project.

For the technological products that a group is charged with creating, there must be a forum to discuss ideas about technical architecture, selection of tools, design details, and aesthetics. For the process and culture of the organization, there should be a similar forum in which it's safe to discuss the approach to the project, the behavior of others, the expectations of individuals and subgroups, roles and responsibilities, schedules, budgets, and all other constraints under which technical projects work.

Then everyone must understand where the appropriate forum is for their ideas. It must be clear that an idea relates to one or more areas of responsibility in order to make sure that ideas are not only expressed but expressed within the right forum.

And once an idea has found the appropriate forum, it must be safe to debate the merits of it aggressively in order to ascertain its true value in relation to other ideas that are also being debated. Geeks must feel free to advocate their positions vociferously without fear of retribution and to abandon their position without shame. The goal of any debate must always be to discover the best idea given the constraints under which any team works.

In these forums, although not everyone in the group may be present, all must feel that their point of view is being advocated and represented effectively. If everyone feels that their ideas have received a fair hearing, whether or not they prevail, they will believe that a fair process has been followed, their ideas have been considered, and a measured judgment has been made. Such a fair process legitimizes decisions in the eyes of the geeks and ensures that the best decisions possible are made.

This is a much less fragile structure than the traditional hierarchical management structure in which a single person is expected to vet all ideas and make decisions. In creating forums for ideas, the group embraces the wisdom of many more people than just the one person who's designated as a leader. At the same time, it raises the commitment and motivation of the group members.

The leader's role in these forums should be to assign members and only rarely to participate in the discussions. It's too easy for everyone in the group to devolve into a position in which the leader makes decisions for everyone.

As an example, I'll describe one of my clients. WidgetSoft (not its real name) was a typical midsized software product company that had grown to about one hundred employees over its twenty-year history. It had many loyal and happy customers but internally was having serious trouble making decisions about setting priorities for which products to enhance when. Each developer would try to decide what he or she thought was most important to fix in the product without consulting with anyone else. When a manager found out what someone was working on, he or she would get upset and tell the developer to work on something else. Decisions were made and unmade constantly. The company also had serious coordination problems. New product releases would be sent out by the product development group, but the help-desk people wouldn't find out about them until a client called with a problem, and the salespeople never found out about the new features that they could be selling.

What had happened to WidgetSoft is quite common. It had tried to retain a hierarchical approach to decision making, but the company had grown too large and president was far too busy to make all the decisions and coordinate all the activities. Instead of creating a forum for conflict and coordination, each department, in isolation from the others, did what it thought was best.

To solve this problem, we created a few cross-departmental groups that took on the responsibility for determining the priorities for product enhancement. These groups had representatives from all the concerned departments, like product development, marketing, support, professional services, and sales. In the group meetings, they would debate the priorities for the products and eventually come to conclusions about what to improve when, given the constraints of time and budget. Not only did these groups make it possible for decisions to be finalized, they also helped coordinate activities and information across departments. Because a representative of each group had taken part in the process, surprises had been eliminated too.

Supporting Conflict Resolution

Once you've created an environment in which people feel free to bring their ideas to an appropriate forum for debate and consideration, it's important also to provide support to the people in these groups to help with conflict resolution. Although ideally all of the debate and conflict within these forums would take place in an open-minded, egoless manner, this is not always the case.

At times, these conflicts become intractable, and someone needs to help break the deadlock. As much as possible, individuals within these decision-making groups should be allowed to resolve their own disputes and learn how to deal with one another and with difficult decisions. But occasionally a conflict goes beyond just making a difficult decision and becomes a counterproductive battle. In these situations, a leader must be able to step in to help resolve the situation without undermining the group's ability to make further decisions in the future.

These intractable conflicts can result from a number of sources. One of the most common is personality conflict. Let's face it. Some people just don't like each other. Their basic behavior patterns and personalities irk each other, and they are unable to get along. If they're both truly committed to achieving a common goal, they may be able to put aside their dislike for one another and work together, but all too often, it isn't enough. In the case of a personality conflict, a leader must be prepared to step in and help the feuding parties learn to deal with one another or separate them.

In other cases, the conflict may be rooted in fundamental disagreements about what is best to do to achieve the group goals. Here a leader must be able to help illuminate the trade-offs and the conflicting assumptions that underlie the differing positions. To be coordinative, he must be able to help the team build its own consensus rather than take decision-making responsibility away from the members. Although the temptation is often to play Solomon and attempt to make a wise decision in a difficult dispute, that reinforces the idea that the group need not debate the issue to conclusion but can lobby the leader for a favorable judgment instead. Once that assumption becomes part of an organizational culture, it's hard to prevent decentralized decision making from collapsing.

When the dispute is based on the ambitions of one or more people rather than what is the best decision for the group, a leader must be prepared to step in and restore the proper basis for decision making. Once self-interested politics becomes the group norm, it's difficult to change it back to a more positive basis.

Valuing Achievement, Not Just Knowledge

Another key to creating a productive environment is ensuring that you avoid one of the greatest traps in knowledge work: the belief that knowledge is more important than achievement. For geeks who are steeped in the details of their technical field, it often seems more important to know things than to apply them. And, certainly, a lot of platitudes reinforce this idea (for example, "Knowledge is power" and "You can never know too much").

Using the tools of recognition and reward, you as a leader have the opportunity to set the tone as to which is more important. Clearly, knowledge expansion has value for an organization, but it must be properly balanced with the productive application of knowledge. Where that balance is struck becomes quickly ingrained in the culture and is difficult to change.

Defining Physical Space

Although geeks live a large part of their lives in their heads, you still need to think about the physical environment in which they work. With all this attention paid to organizational and political structure, it may seem easy to overlook the contribution of the physical environment to the productivity of the geek group. That would be a mistake.

The physical work space for a technical team must be appropriate given the nature of geekwork. Geeks need quiet, private areas for individual concentration when working alone. They also need enclosed gathering spaces for formal and informal conversation to ensure the smooth flow of information. Some of the gathering points should be out in the open, such as a kitchen or playroom, to encourage dialogue during happenstance meetings. Other common spaces should be enclosed, where people can have spirited debates without fear of disturbing others or being overheard inappropriately.

All too often, I see programmers in bullpen areas, with eight to ten people crammed into an undivided work space where they attempt to concentrate. Any conversation interrupts all of them. This situation typically results in major productivity losses. Putting three to four people in a small space can be conducive to good communication if they are all working on tightly connected parts of a system, but usually it just leads to inefficiency due to interruptions in thought and concentration.

It's also important for a leader to recognize the symbolic nature of space and the effects it has on the culture of a group. If everyone associated with the project has identical cubicles, it communicates something very different about status and hierarchy than if junior people work in the bullpen, managers get cubicles, and executives have offices with doors and windows. The more status conscious the space allocation appears, the more status will be an important feature in the culture. And when status becomes too important, ideas and information flow less efficiently, diminishing the quality and quantity of geekwork that can be done.

Being the Therapist

The chaos, pressure, stress, and ambiguity of geekwork take a toll on project teams that sometimes presents itself as emotional distress. When this happens, someone has got to be there to help patch people up so that they can resolve their issues just enough to get back on the front lines. Dealing with minor mental health issues is another part of providing internal facilitation.

Usually it falls to leaders to take on this crucial role. Sometimes there are multiple people within an office who serve in this unofficial and unnamed function. Occasionally, organizations hire consultants to help out. (One of my clients jokingly calls me Sydney because he treats me like the psychiatrist character on the television show M*A*S*H who shows up occasionally to help patch people's heads together so they can get on with the war. Like the television characters, he calls me only to help out with the tough cases.)

The types of issues can range from the simple and silly to the significant and profound. Employees are people and have real emotions and real lives. Sometimes the therapist just needs to listen to complaints and let a geek blow off steam. Other times, she needs to help a person learn to manage stress. Often, stress will lead people to revert to dysfunctional behaviors that ordinarily don't show up but do appear under pressure.

Sometimes people experience more than just minor stress-related behavioral problems. They face major life crises like the death of a family member or divorce. One of the most important parts of being the office therapist is to know when someone needs more help than you are qualified to offer and to help that person find professional help without fear or shame.

Facilitating Tasks

The other part of internal facilitation involves coordination of day-to-day tasks that comprise the bulk of geekwork. While this may seem a less lofty side of geek leadership, it is no less important. Technology teams waste tremendous amounts of energy in internal friction through uncoordinated work, duplicated efforts, and wasted time.

Leaders' ability to keep all team members working at peak efficiency and heading in the same direction is just as critical to successful management of geek groups as are the other tasks of leadership.

Allocating Resources

Among the most important and subtle duties of the geek leader is that of allocating resources to projects and tasks: assigning people to project roles, allocating equipment and funds to projects, hiring consultants and contractors, and acquiring and distributing training.

Although this may seem like a simple administrative duty, resource allocation lies at the heart of every geek organization. The results of the decisions made in resource allocation affect every aspect of the organization and its output. For example, the selection of who will be assigned to which project clearly affects the skills balance on a project team, the culture of the team, and the quality of the projects' product. But it also affects the career progression of each person on the project, the morale of the project team, and the entire organization's employee retention rate.

The geek leader must strive to expand the ability to allocate resources better, constantly trying to expand the range of factors considered when trying to balance the needs of the organization, the skills of individuals, the mix of teams, the client relationship, the aspirations of individual geeks, and cost and time constraints.

Among all the skills for personal productivity that a geek leader must develop, resource allocation may not be at the very top of a list, but it is certainly in the top class of important skills to have.

Coordinating Schedules

Within a working group, geeks should be able to coordinate their own schedules with one another without any outside assistance. And theoretically, one working group should be able to coordinate its interdependencies and schedules with other working groups through a liaison function. It doesn't always work out that way.

Because most geeks are introverts, it pays to monitor interteam communication and coordination to make sure that schedules and interdependencies are being properly planned. Often projects' milestone deadlines change but are not universally communicated, and when one group doesn't receive something it needs from another group on time, dead time can result, wasting both funds and time.

As projects progress, the geek leader must monitor schedule slips for both their magnitude and their effects on other teams. When it becomes clear that there's a disconnect between two or more team schedules, the leader must bring the parties together to ensure that their schedules are reconciled appropriately.

As part of reconciling schedules, it's important to maintain the blame-free environment, focusing on planning for the future rather than assessing blame for the past. All too often, schedule changes become flash points for interteam rivalries, with each team blaming the other for its own inability to meet a schedule. Once the situation deteriorates to the point of blaming one another for missing the deadline, all the emotional and intellectual energy goes into assessing blame rather than trying to figure out the best course of action.

Coordinating Tasks

In addition to coordinating the schedules among work groups, the geek leader must ensure that all appropriate tasks are being covered. Usually, related groups work together to ensure that all necessary tasks are being completed by someone, but occasionally, especially on projects with tight deadlines, things sometimes fall through the cracks and get missed.

Part of the geek leader's oversight responsibilities is to ensure that all necessary tasks have a responsible party that will take care it. This is not to say that the geek leader needs to delegate tasks directly to groups, but only to recognize and publicize the unattended need and ensure that it is appropriately claimed. If no one steps up and accepts responsibility for the need, it may become necessary to assign it.

You should also be on the lookout for duplicated efforts, where multiple groups take responsibility for the same tasks but fail to coordinate with each other. In these situations, it's much easier to step in to coordinate a resolution. Geeks rarely complain when someone from above steps in to help eliminate duplicative work, whereas they may resist when confronted with more work.

Overcoming Obstacles

Another critical role that a geek leader plays in coordinating tasks is helping individuals and teams overcome obstacles to success. Although project teams can usually resolve their own issues, occasionally they need outside help. A number of things can come up during projects that end up in a leader's lap, and if no one helps out with them, projects stall, schedules slip, geeks get frustrated and sometimes quit, and budgets are blown.

The most common problems for leaders to resolve are resource constraints: equipment or software scarcity, technical or managerial skills deficit, office space deficiency, or personnel shortage. If a leader already has resources to resolve the problem, he helps with allocation. If he doesn't have them available, he will typically use his role as outside representative to acquire the necessary resources to resolve the problem. The next most common obstacle is the schedule slip. A leader can handle this in several ways, including resource acquisition or allocation, negotiating project scope reduction, or bargaining with clients for more time.

The danger of helping teams overcome their obstacles is that if a leader is too eager to help, geeks may become dependent on the leader and no longer try to solve their own problems. Teams need a leader who will help them overcome obstacles but only ones that are intractable for the team alone.

Monitoring Effectiveness

Although the geek leader may not control projects in the classical sense, she must continue to monitor them and provide advice and direction when necessary. Providing leadership and guidance is not the same thing as oversight and control.

Although in theory self-directed teams are capable of detecting and resolving their own problems, a leader must nevertheless maintain overall responsibility for project oversight. Teams should be monitored for their effectiveness so that appropriate and timely interventions can be arranged when necessary to keep people and projects on track.

Monitoring a team does not mean micromanaging its activities. In her Harvard Business School course "Power and Influence," Linda Hill identifies three things that need to be monitored to keep tabs on project teams:

- Is this team delivering its product or service within the expected time, quality, and budgetary constraints?

- Is the experience for the team members generally positive, enhancing their knowledge and future prospects?

- Will the people on this team be able to work together in the future?[1]

If the answer to any of these questions is no, you as a leader must decide whether an intervention should be arranged to help the team functionally or organizationally. Sometimes all that's required is gentle prodding and a reminder of their priorities; at other times, more dramatic intervention is needed.

Arranging Interventions

When you discover that a work team is not progressing satisfactorily, it falls to you as leader to prescribe an appropriate intervention. Interventions can take many forms, ranging from brief review meetings to complete project reorganizations with staffing changes or even project cancellations.

Interventions of this sort can result in dramatic performance improvements for struggling teams but can also have little effect or even negative consequences should they be done inappropriately. Choosing to intervene in an ongoing project or department is a serious matter that should not be taken lightly. These interventions have both costs and benefits and can be very risky, sometimes making things worse rather than better.

The first difficult question is what sort of intervention is appropriate. Should a diagnostic review be done of the technical output, the team process, the organizational structure and dynamics, or all three? And regardless of the scope of the review, should it be done by internal personnel or consultants? Should it be done in a coaching exploratory manner or as a more comprehensive and formal audit?

Regardless of which choices are made, there are always costs for arranging intervention. At a minimum, the team loses significant productivity as the review is conducted. Usually teams view an intervention as some sort of punishment for perceived failure, and team morale suffers temporarily. If the intervention is successful, morale is quickly restored. In cases where an intervention fails, morale can be decimated for long periods of time.

One of the biggest dangers is to intervene too soon. Although it can be difficult to watch a group struggle with its own problems, geek groups often resolve their own issues relatively quickly. You'll have to use your professional judgment as to whether the risks of an intervention outweigh the risks of waiting.

When you intervene too soon, you often interrupt a resolution that's already in progress. When this happens, you may delay or derail a solution, undermine the mutual trust between you and the team, damage the group's ability to work together in the future, or initiate a culture of obfuscation and blame.

But despite all these warnings, teams do need interventions more often than we would like. Given how few technical projects succeed, it pays to be alert since many problems can be addressed quickly and easily when discovered early.

As an example, I'll describe another client. Wisenheimer (again, not its real name) was a very large organization, with tens of thousands of employees. When it decided to start work on a Web site that customers could use to view and change their personal information, it hired a reputable consulting firm to help out. The project was expected to cost over $2 million and last over a year. After only a few weeks, the executive responsible for the group was already feeling uneasy about the progress and called me in to check things out. He wasn't familiar with the details but just had a bad feeling. So once a week, I started joining the team status meeting, learning about what they were doing.

After the first meeting, it was clear that both the employees of Wisenheimer and the consultants had become completely captivated by the technical architectural details of how some aspect of peak-load balancing would be handled. Unfortunately, they hadn't yet explicitly defined *what* the system would do before they were trying to figuring *how* it would do it. Clearly, this was a problem, so at the first meeting, I suggested that they put aside these details until later in the project. At the following meeting, this technical gewgaw was still the only thing on the agenda. Again I suggested that this consideration be put off. But their obsession was not easily put aside.

When I arrived at the fourth meeting and was handed the paper with the agenda showing technical architecture as the only item again, I stood up, ripped the paper in half, and told them not to waste their money on me or their $2 million on the project. I politely but forcefully suggested they cancel the whole thing rather than continue on this way. That got their attention.

By the next week, the team had pulled back from their fascination with the architecture and had started on what they should have been doing in the first place: figuring out precisely what the system needed to do.

Streaming Information

The final role that a geek leader plays in internal coordination is that of information source. In addition to setting the tone for the value of openly shared information, you must constantly make efforts to share information yourself. As someone who has access to considerable detailed information about what's taking place within the group as well as outside the group, you should be constantly making an effort to share information.

As you stream information to the group, not only will they begin to share information more freely among themselves but they will also develop trust and respect for your leadership role. Although geeks are by nature mistrustful of authority, they can be quite appreciative of people who bring them the information and resources they need to be successful in their work.

Summary

FUNDAMENTAL QUESTIONS

- How do geek leaders provide internal facilitation?
- What's the difference between control and facilitation?
- What issues should be considered when establishing geekwork environments?
- What issues should be considered when coordinating the tasks of geekwork?

KEY IDEAS

- A leader's role within a geek group is mostly to facilitate the flow of ideas and activities rather than the more traditional approach of command and control.
- There are two categories of things that leaders must facilitate: establishing and maintaining environment and coordinating tasks.
- Leaders who resist the futility of power lose power through the resistance of geeks.
- Leaders who embrace the facilitation role gain power by controlling the agenda and the flow of information.

8

Furnishing External Representation

Some of the responsibilities of geek leaders are similar to those of leaders in more conventional environments. External representation is one that carries over relatively unaltered by the context of geek leadership.

Just as the president of the United States represents all American citizens when meeting with the president of France to discuss matters of international trade or as the pope represents all Catholics when meeting with the head of the Eastern Orthodox church to discuss matters of interchurch dialogue, geek leaders represent the geeks in their organization when meeting with non-geeks from other areas of the company, external vendors, customers, or the media.

Representing geeks to the outside world plays an important role in determining whether a group will be successful and prosperous. When representation is done well, the leader can bring information, resources, and attention to the technical group. When it is done poorly, he can bring disdain, scorn, and scarcity of resources.

Representing geeks should be viewed as a high honor for geek leaders. In this role, you have an opportunity to establish an appropriate image for yourself and those you represent. But a geek leader also has the responsibility to use the representation function to further the interest of geeks and ensure that their needs and aspirations become part of the organization's debate over policy and strategy.

Functions of Representation

Representing geeks to the outside world is much more than an opportunity to do lunch or hobnob with the elite. It serves many functions for the successful operation of geek groups and in many ways plays a determining role in the success of geekwork. The responsibilities that come with representation are these:

- Acquiring information
- Establishing and maintaining alignment
- Obtaining resources
- Managing expectations
- Projecting prominence
- Protecting geeks
- Insulating geeks
- Attracting geeks

Acquiring Information

The first need that a geek leader's representation role fills is that of information. To some extent, every group needs an intelligence operation that collects the information it requires to plan its activities successfully and avoid costly mistakes. But rather than have agencies equipped with spy satellites, wire-taps, moles, and double agents, you'll be working in a more low-tech fashion like a scout, who looks out ahead and brings information back to the group.

Given the diversity of circumstances and situations, it's not possible to come up with a comprehensive list of information that you'll need to gather and redistribute as part of your internal coordination function. Here are a few of the key pieces of information that typically are needed to maintain a successful technology group:

- *Future business plans.* If you are trying to build a product for sale to a customer base, you need a constant flow of information about the competitive environment, the basis of competition, and planned and anticipated changes to the business strategy of your clients. If you are building custom applications for an internal business unit, you need information on its plans, as well as its competitive information.

- *The political landscape.* Although I don't recommend playing political games yourself, it's always important to understand what others in the organization are up to. Without knowing the current issues under debate, the positions of the key players, the dynamics of coalition building, and the likely outcomes, you'll be completely unprepared when strategic, organizational, or tactical changes arise.

- *The technological landscape.* Although there may be others in the organization who also monitor the external technical environment for new products, new standards, or product retirements, geek leaders also pay attention to management and technology trends in order to guide the conversation about internal plans.

- *Client attitudes, expectations, and impressions.* Geek leaders stay in touch with the opinions and expectations that clients hold about their group and technologies. Whether your clients are internal or external, it's always important to know how satisfied they are with your products and services.

- *The sociopolitical and economic environment.* Geek leaders recognize the broader context in which their group, company, and even industry exist and monitor information about events and trends that may affect the group.

Establishing and Maintaining Alignment

The information that you gather is not just for entertainment or enrichment. It serves as the basis for aligning geeks and geekwork with the needs and goals of the clients, both internal and external.

Alignment is about fit—that is, the mutually supportive relationships among the goals, technologies, and processes of an organization and project. Groups that exhibit good alignment are constantly being fine-tuned to ensure that all the elements of products and services are internally consistent and mutually reinforcing. Here are some of the factors that need to be aligned:

- Business problems being solved or opportunities being exploited
- Technical solutions to the problems
- Budgets, schedules, and quality constraints on projects
- Goals of geeks
- Goals of client constituencies
- Future applicability of the solutions
- Implementation approaches

Alignment does not imply blindly accepting externally imposed direction and goals, but engaging as a full participant in setting business strategy representing geeks' interests and perspectives. Alignment is not a one-time event but an ongoing process to ensure that the best priorities have been established for the overall organization.

A geek leader's representation role in alignment is to be an advocate for the contributions of geeks and technology to overall organizational strategy decisions. Participating in alignment means more than just accepting and filling orders for technical gewgaws; it also encompasses exploring strategic opportunities made possible by technology that would otherwise go unnoticed.

Obtaining Resources

Another function of external representation is that of hunter-gatherer—that is, seeking out and acquiring the resources necessary for the group to be successful. You must get out into the corporate savanna and locate, fight for, and acquire the resources geeks need. These needs fall into several categories:

- *Budget.* The most important resource a leader can bring to the group is cash. As the single most flexible resource, it can be used to acquire most of the others.

- *People.* Whether acquiring permanent staff or temporary contractors, the most important resource in knowledge work is knowledgeable people. You've got to bring back a mix of people with the appropriate skills and temperaments to make projects successful.

- *Equipment.* There's always a battle over capital spending, especially on high-tech items that are obsolete before the packaging peanuts hit the floor after opening the box. But without equipment, time is wasted, which is generally more expensive in both real costs and opportunity costs than equipment.

- *Physical space.* The quality and quantity of physical space can have dramatic effects on the productivity of geeks. Some projects that have all the money, people, and equipment they need flounder due to poor environment quality.

- *Test data.* For highly complex corporate systems, it's critical that new systems be tested with realistic data, although data can be hard to reproduce manually. These data are often difficult to acquire because they haven't been previously captured, exist only in corrupted form, or there are security concerns.

- *Client attention.* Many projects become misaligned because the client and users are too busy with their day-to-day jobs to ensure that things are on track. At the end of the process, they finally show up and point out problems that could have been addressed early on in the process.

Managing Expectations

Geek leaders are responsible for helping to ensure client satisfaction in part by limiting customer expectations to realistic levels. As with alignment, this is not a one-time event but a constant struggle that must be managed throughout the project life cycle.

At the outset of projects, client expectations are often at their peak, when grandiose visions of the benefits of technology have yet to crash on the rocks of hard reality. It's often difficult for leaders to rein in expectations at this point because they don't want to limit their effectiveness at acquiring resources to devote to the project. Leaders may allow clients' unrealistic expectations to grow unchecked at the outset of a project in order to gain the support necessary to launch the effort, believing that they can manage them once things have started. But in fact, this sort of bait-and-switch approach rarely works, and in the long run it diminishes mutual trust between leaders and customers, as well as between geeks and leaders.

Even if expectations are properly managed at the outset of a project, they must be constantly monitored and corrected as a project progresses. Invariably, the scope of a project changes over time, expanding here and shrinking there until eventually solidifying. As these changes occur, it's important to keep the client informed to avoid any surprise at the end of a project.

Perhaps most important, customer expectations should be managed at the end of a project to ensure that the product and services delivered meet or exceed expectations. The final impressions left by the end stages of a project serve as a basis for an ongoing relationship. In successful projects where expectations are managed realistically, a long-term bond of mutual trust and respect can be formed. When expectations are managed only at the end of the process, if at all, clients believe that geeks are deceptive and not to be trusted.

No matter how many people within the technology organization talk to clients, your interactions as a leader carry the most weight and set the tone for the overall relationship.

Projecting Prominence

Geek leaders function as symbols to outsiders, a representation of the entire geek organization and the guardian of its image both inside and outside the company. The impression you project becomes a proxy in the minds of outsiders for the character of geeks individually and as a group and the quality of their work. In this role, you become responsible in large measure for how the group is viewed and the prestige the members hold.

The esteem in which you are personally held directly affects the prestige that you bring to the group. It is a function of both the form and substance of your interaction with outsiders. It can be affected by a number of your attributes:

- *Expertise.* The knowledge you display about both business and technology and their complementary nature can have a strong effect on how others view you. Since, in general, outsiders don't have the expertise to know how knowledgeable you are about technical subjects, they judge you in part by how knowledgeable you appear to be about their field of expertise where they are more capable of making judgments.

- *Integrity.* If you develop a reputation for honesty in your dealings with the outside world, that perception will typically reflect on all the geeks in your organization. If you're seen as deceitful, devious, or secretive, that too will carry over to others.

- *Forthrightness.* If you are viewed as direct, open, and forthcoming with information you bring to others, you will be trusted and rewarded with information in return. If you are viewed as secretive or aloof, you will have a tough time getting information and will reduce the prestige of the group.

- *Insight.* If you display extraordinary insight about the relationship between business and technology, human nature, and the dynamics of your organization, you will be positioned to be accepted as a leader in the whole organization rather than merely as a service provider to the rest of the company.

- *Articulateness.* No matter how smart, capable, honest, and insightful you are, if you are unable to communicate effectively in the language of outsiders, no one will ever know.

- *Reputation.* If you are known beyond the boundaries of your own organization, write articles for magazines, are quoted in newspapers, write books, or hold prominent positions in industry associations, both you and your geek organization take on legitimacy and glamour far greater than ordinarily accorded technology groups.

• *Charisma*. Your general ability to be liked by others as well as respected reflects on everyone under your guidance.

Clearly, how well you handle the other functions of representation also have a direct effect on how you are viewed by others. The more capably you handle the other functions, the greater will be the esteem in which the geek organization will be held.

Protecting Geeks

A representative also protects geeks from the dangers of the outside world. The role of protector manifests itself in several different ways and serves a number of purposes:

• *Geek advocate*. First and foremost, someone needs to represent the needs and aspirations of geeks to the broader organization, both articulating and advocating for them. Not only is it important to the organization that this perspective be adequately represented, but geeks must also feel that they have an active champion who cares about what they want and need.

• *Political insulation*. Geeks need to be protected from the whimsical nature of self-interested politics that may be taking place elsewhere in the organization. If their creative energy and attention are drawn to internal political games, less will be available for geek-work, diminishing productivity and morale.

• *Change buffer*. Like all other organizations, geek groups must respond to their dynamic environment with appropriate change, but change has its costs and must be measured out at the right times and in the right ways to minimize lost productivity and emotional discomfort. A geek leader protects others from unnecessary change, selecting appropriate times to introduce it.

In addition to filling these organizational purposes, protection improves the morale of geeks. If they feel they work in an organization with a strong and active advocate, they're more likely to form a bond with both the leader and the organization. If they feel abandoned to the whims of the world, then they will believe that they can trust only themselves.

Insulating Geeks

In addition to protecting the group from the forces of the outside world, the geek leader provides insulation to ensure that the group remains productive. Whereas protection prevents geeks from suffering the ill effects of events and attitudes in their surroundings, insulation diminishes the intensity of their contact with the outside world. This is not to say that geeks should be insensitive to the rest of the organization, but they do require a certain distance to allow them to be productive by concentrating on geekwork.

Working in some organizations is like living in an echo chamber, where even the tiniest sound bounces from place to place and person to person, reverberating constantly throughout the company. In places like this, the rumor mill is so active that it can serve as a constant interruption and distraction. In other places, it becomes the primary conduit through which vital information passes.

Because geekwork requires focused concentration, interruptions are often much more costly than the value of the information passed would warrant. The geek leader must serve as a buffer, providing an appropriate measure of insulation that will dampen the sounds and distractions while not completely isolating geeks from the rest of the company.

Attracting Geeks

The final function of external representation is that of attracting others to the organization. A leader's ability to recruit capable, talented, and compatible personnel at all levels of the organization is critical to the health of almost any geek group. To attract appropriate new people to the organization, a geek leader must work on a number of levels:

- *Acquiring resources.* In addition to pay and benefits, space, equipment, technology, and other resources serve to help attract talent.
- *Identifying needs.* A geek leader identifies the skill deficits within an organization to ascertain the types of people needed. This includes more than just technical skills or project management skills; it also encompasses business skills, leadership skills, relationship building skills, and teamwork skills.
- *Drawing a compelling picture.* Geek leaders explain the organization to candidates in a compelling way that demonstrates how the environment will fill their needs while also filling the needs of the organization.
- *Locating appropriate people.* A geek leader can provide significant creativity in seeking out candidates. More than just running ads in newspapers or hiring friends of employees, he guides hands-on recruiters in finding other companies from which to poach talent, universities with pools of potential talent, and international sources for personnel.
- *Discerning cultural fit.* Finding good candidates is more than just identifying people with appropriate skills and convincing them to join the organization. It also requires a deep understanding of the culture of the work environment, as well as the ability to foresee how a particular candidate would fit in.

Even in organizations that are not growing, the geek leader cannot afford to ignore the importance of recruiting to the success of the group. Geek turnover within technology organizations has remained at high levels for decades when compared with other corporate departments, so recruiting is always important.

Internal Relationships

The next question we must ask is, "To whom do geeks need representation?" There are two answers. First, they need to be represented to other internal groups within the company and, second, to external organizations and individuals.

When representing geeks within the organization, there are two categories of relationships to consider: laterally to peer organizations and upward to senior management.

Peer Organizations

In most companies, the IT department represents a centralized service provided to all the other departments within the organization. Occasionally, in companies where technology or technologically enabled services are part of the product and not just part of the infrastructure of the company, IT also plays an important role in product development. In both cases, geeks working within the organization can usually identify many constituencies that qualify as clients or users of their technology. Most of the people identified as clients will be from peer groups rather than higher up on the organization chart.

Maintaining strong relations with peer organizations falls primarily to geek leaders, who represent the technology group to these peers. There are several issues on which the peers must collaborate to build consensus for action within the broader organization:

• *Alignment.* Since most of the systems developed, deployed, and maintained by IT departments are used by peer organizations, it's critical that the goals, projects, and directions are consistently aligned between the technology group and the various user groups, such as sales, marketing, manufacturing, distribution, accounting, finance, or purchasing. Forging alignment often requires multilateral negotiations between multiple peer groups and the technology department.

- *Resources*. When IT groups offer services to peer organizations, resource discussions are often necessary to agree on budget, space, personnel, and the participation of personnel from user departments.
- *Strategy*. As each department within a large organization pursues its own agenda, new organizational strategies often emerge without conscious decisions. They accumulate slowly based on the confluence of numerous tactical decisions, but when they are combined, they form a pattern of behavior that can be recognized as a business strategy. Because many innovative business strategies require technology to enable them, the representative of the technology department may be drawn into strategic conversations. Similarly, new ideas may also come not from the business unit but from the technology department itself and be offered as options to the business unit.

Upward Relationships

The second category of internal relationships that must be managed by the geek leader is relationships with executives in the organization. These may include direct reporting relationships such as to a CEO or CFO or relationships to general executives or board members.

Regardless of whether the relationship includes direct reporting, the geek leader is responsible for maintaining support for the technical group within the upper reaches of the organization. Without support, the technology group is likely to become an organizational backwater, a permanent cost center viewed as a burden rather than a strategic asset.

Geek leaders need to understand how senior management views the role of technology in the organization and whether they consider it important to the company's future. They need to understand the views of each individual in senior management and not just the current consensus in order to build effective support.

Geek leaders need to understand senior management's expectations of both the technology organization as a whole and the geek leader personally. A geek leader works to build constructive relationships with senior management on a personal level in order to be an effective advocate.

External Relationships

Geek leaders forge effective links with the world outside the company representing the needs and interests of those inside the organization. There are a number of categories of interaction with the outside world to which a geek leader must pay attention.

Customers

Especially when technology is either part of the product or enables core services to be delivered to customers, geek leaders may be drawn in to direct contact with the company's customers. This may take the form of occasional informal interaction with key customers or may be a regular part of the job.

For some projects, customer input may be sought to help define user needs as part of the system design process. Although the customer meetings are typically run by more junior analysts, geek leaders may get involved in arranging these interactions and need to be sensitive to setting proper expectations about the degree of effect that direct consumer opinions will have on the detailed design of a product. Allowing customers to believe that anything they wish for will be placed in the product or service is a promise of future disappointment and poor customer satisfaction.

Recruiting

Although most geek leaders don't usually do recruiting by themselves, they still have important roles to play as a representative of the organization to the community of recruiting professionals as well as the candidate pool in general. In the long run, one of the biggest influences a leader can have on a group is through recruiting. Bringing new blood into an organization is an opportunity to shape its character, values, and size. Adding new people to the organization and retaining them often makes the most lasting change a leader can make, more enduring than any policy or incentive.

As a representative to the recruiting community, a geek leader sets the tone for the type of people he wants added to the organization. More than just identifying particular technological skill sets, he becomes involved in describing the human characteristics of the types of people to recruit.

To do this, he must be articulate about management skills, relationship skills, teamwork skills, leadership characteristics, and other soft skills. It's not enough just to tell recruiters, "I want a new project manager." You've got to be able to speak precisely about organizational skills, communication skills, attitudes toward users and subordinates, willingness to share information and credit, ability to negotiate, listening skills, energy and drive, sources of motivation, values, adaptability, and other difficult-to-define characteristics.

When communicating these sorts of things to recruiters, a geek leader must be willing to back up the importance of these skills by refusing to hire people who have the right technical skills but don't match the soft characteristics. Recruiters will often try to convince you to hire someone who has the technical skills but is not a cultural fit. If you allow this to happen, you will demonstrate your lack of commitment to cultural criteria as a barrier to entry to the group and lose control of this critical function.

And finally as a representative, especially in cases when recruiting very senior personnel, a geek leader may be personally involved in the recruiting process. Here you must project an appropriate image of the organization to attract individuals whom you'd like to add.

Media

Depending on the organization and the product you're working with, a geek leader may have an opportunity or need to have a relationship with the print or electronic media. If so, this is a wonderful opportunity both to represent yourself and your organization to the world and to boost the prestige of geeks in your organization.

External Vendors

Technology groups have always had strong relationships with outside vendors for hardware, operating systems, and software tools. Although some of these relationships represent only short-term transactions, many of them require long-term relationships that involve substantial sums of money. In these cases, geek leaders often get involved in setting the tone of the relationship, as well as managing major negotiations and critical problems.

It has become increasingly common for technology groups both large and small to rely heavily on outside vendors for services as well as products. In some cases, these outsourcing contracts can account for the vast majority of departmental budgets when a single supplier is responsible for all custom programming, maintenance and support of key applications, and systems. But even in smaller cases, consultants and contractors often provide the bulk of work on major development and deployment projects.

In addition, a geek leader often becomes involved in establishing new relationships with vendors, managing ongoing relationships, negotiating contracts, handling crises and disputes, and terminating relationships. In all these situations, he is representing both the entire organization and the geeks within it.

Summary

Fundamental Questions
- How do geek leaders represent geeks to outside organizations and individuals?
- Why is external representation important?
- To whom do geek leaders represent geeks?

KEY IDEAS

- Part of a leader's role is to buffer geek groups from the outside world.

- In representing geek groups, leaders provide a number of important functions.

- Geek leaders represent geek groups to many constituencies both internal and external to the organization.

9

Managing Ambiguity

The fourth and perhaps most important responsibility of a geek leader is to manage ambiguity. In this most subtle of the responsibilities, a geek leader manages ambiguity at three levels simultaneously, juggling issues of structure, environment, and task.

Geek leaders themselves need a high tolerance for ambiguity and an ability to be productive in the absence of clarity. They need to maintain composure and help others to do so in situations clouded by confusion. The ability to help an entire group make sense of its environment and activities lies at the very core of a leader's role.

What Is Ambiguity?

Ambiguity is the opposite of clarity. To think about something with complete clarity, you need to have a total command of all the facts about it and also understand the meanings of all the facts. Something is ambiguous if you are unaware of it altogether, have incomplete information about it, or don't understand its implications or meanings.

When you think about the state of your knowledge about the world—its past and future, nature and the works of humanity—you can evaluate it all on a simple two-dimensional scale (see Figure 9.1), with clarity on one end and ambiguity at the other end.

Things about which you feel that you have absolute knowledge—certainty about not only the facts but their meanings—you place on the clarity end of the scale (point D). Things about which you have limited knowledge of either facts or their meanings might fall somewhere in the middle (point C). Things that you know exist but are uncertain of the facts or their meanings might fall toward the ambiguity side (point B). And things about which you may be totally ignorant of the facts or their meanings appear at the ambiguous end of the scale (point A).

In general, most things fall somewhere in between the poles. You neither have all the facts and meanings, nor do you completely lack knowledge about them. Most things you know about are at least a bit ambiguous.

Geekwork, by its nature, falls toward the ambiguous side of this scale. Geekwork is largely about the creation and application of technical ideas, identifying and solving new problems or solving old problems in new and creative ways. What could be more ambiguous than creativity? You start out without even knowing what problem you're working on, and when you do finally discover what the problem is, then you have to figure out how to solve it. The entire process is designed to find and resolve ambiguity. So ambiguity is also an integral part of the problem-solution mind-set.

Ambiguity Organizes Geekwork

The problem-solution thinking pattern so common in geeks reminds us that geekwork is all about ambiguity. Problems are mysteries that we do not yet know a solution to. Even discovering the right problems to address is a mystery. Usually, we think of

FIGURE 9.1. Clarity Versus Ambiguity Scale.

functional specialties as being based on knowledge and expertise, that is, on what we do know. Ironically, the geekwork form of knowledge work is organized by what we don't know.

The structures of projects and departments are designed to channel the discovery of questions and their solutions through the application of specialized knowledge. When a project starts, the team members don't really know what they are going to do. They don't even completely understand what questions they are going to be expected to answer, what experiments they are going to have to do. If they are lucky, they do know from what perspective they are expected to approach the discovery and resolution of questions. That's all.

If you fail to understand the fundamental effects of ambiguity on geekwork, you will have a very hard time organizing work productively.

The Hierarchy of Ambiguity

To manage ambiguity, you have to understand that ambiguity itself has a structure. It may seem strange at first to think that what you don't know has an inherent structure, but I have developed a model, the Hierarchy of Ambiguity, that represents a categorization of the types of issues and questions that naturally arise related to geekwork. There are three fundamental categories of ambiguity to manage to create an environment in which geeks can be productive: task, structural, and environmental. The purpose of using these categories is to help you make more sense of the chaos that is geekwork and help you identify issues that you are not yet grappling with but should be (see Figure 2 in Part Two introduction, page 101).

• *Environmental ambiguity.* Environmental ambiguity encompasses the lofty questions about how things fit together—about how the world, marketplace, organization, customers, geeks, and geekwork all relate to one another. It thus deals with issues of meaning, purpose, and identity.

Geek leaders are central players in an organization's attempts to make sense of its environment and to establish a coherent identity. Managing environmental ambiguity has a direct effect on an organization's motivation level, strategic direction, values, and culture.

• *Structural ambiguity.* Structural ambiguity encompasses a range of questions about a smaller scope of issues related to the local organization only. These are pragmatic but important questions about what work will be done and how geeks will be organized to do that work. These questions revolve around issues related to projects and processes.

Geek leaders establish order and structure to ensure that geek-work being done is organized to meet the goals and commitments of the group. Structure ensures that efforts are channeled into productive work, and processes are designed to ensure that work is completed and coordinated.

• *Task ambiguity.* Task ambiguity encompasses questions about how individuals and small groups carry out their specific tasks. These are the day-to-day questions about roles, assignments, and judgments.

Geek leaders manage task ambiguity to help individuals be productive and help them understand their roles in project work. Geek leaders also help set standards for performance and behavior with the judgments that they offer.

The remainder of this chapter focuses on the first and most abstract level of ambiguity that geek leaders manage, environmental ambiguity (see Figure 9.2). Of the three levels of ambiguity, this one may seem the most unfamiliar and vague, but don't dismiss its importance in delivering geekwork. It encompasses issues related to the big picture, to interpreting the entire organization and its surroundings. In many types of work, it may not be essential for leaders and employees to develop a common view of the world in order to be productive, but this is not the case in most technical environments. A common understanding of issues related to environmental ambiguity provides a critical foundation for geekwork.

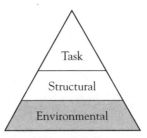

FIGURE 9.2. The Hierarchy of Ambiguity.

What Is Environmental Ambiguity?

Issues related to environmental ambiguity are big, broad questions that tie together the world at the highest level that an organization attempts to interpret and deal with a broad array of global concerns—for example:

- Who are we?
- Why are we here?
- How do we fit into and relate to the outside world?
- What is the significance of our work?
- What are the ethical standards to which we should be held?

Answering these questions helps geeks understand the both the environment and the purpose of an organization, an essential foundation for their work. This information helps guide the technical and managerial decisions that they must make every day as part of designing, developing, deploying, and supporting technology.

Resolving environmental ambiguity also provides more than just background information. Geeks need this information for more than just satisfying curiosity and guiding decisions. It is also essential for meeting their emotional and psychological needs. The worldview developed serves as a foundation for establishing identity and imbuing work with meaning.

In traditional work environments, managers often assume that workers need to understand only their task in order to be productive. Too much information, they think, may be confusing or distracting. They believe that if workers have clear direction and well-aligned incentives, they should have all they need to do their jobs.

In geekwork, this approach doesn't work. The interpretation of the environment serves as the informational bedrock that supports leaders' efforts to nurture motivation, provide internal coordination, and furnish external representation.

Making Sense of the Environment

If some of the questions of environmental ambiguity sound familiar, they should. You may remember that the Context of Geek Leadership model describes the basic relationships among geeks, leaders, geekwork, the organizational environment, and the wider sociopolitical and economic environment. At the center of the model, geeks, leaders, and geekwork form an inseparable three-way relationship—the tripartite relationship. Environmental ambiguity deals with questions about the outer circles of the Context of Geek Leadership, the organizational and sociopolitical environment (see Figure 1.1 on page 14). In short, managing environmental ambiguity is all about setting the tripartite relationship in its broader context.

One of a geek leader's most important responsibilities is to interpret reality—to help followers make sense of the cacophony of hype, facts, opinions, rumors, ideas, and concepts that swirl around the workplace. In part, leaders become leaders by demonstrating the ability to make sense of the world and communicate their understandings to followers in compelling ways. Leaders have to make sense of the environment to chart the visionary course.

As leaders develop coherent understandings, they judge how to communicate them to their followers. Depending on the audience, this can be quite easy or rather complex. Geeks vary widely in the breadth of information that they absorb about the environment. In general, younger people understand and are satisfied with less information about the business and cultural environment than are more senior people. Determining the range of information is part of a leader's responsibility to communicate his interpretations in ways that are both understandable and compelling.

In order to communicate a reasonable picture of the environment, a leader may have to collect, interpret, and disseminate information on a wide variety of topics about the organizational and the sociopolitical environments. This may mean:

- Framing organizational culture
- Identifying political issues and factions
- Anticipating the organization's responses to its environment
- Describing the industry
- Identifying customers
- Characterizing competition
- Analyzing stakeholders
- Detecting technical trends

Making sense of the environment is not a one-time activity. Leaders constantly monitor new information and the ideas of others to validate or disconfirm their own. They must not be afraid to revise or completely change their interpretations, since failure to recognize environmental change is one of the most common ways to marginalize an enterprise. Both slow and steady or rapid discontinuous change can undermine ideas about the environment, leaving organizations vulnerable to competitors.

In his Pulitzer Prize–winning book *The Soul of a New Machine*, Tracy Kidder beautifully captured the story of the creation of Data General's Eclipse MV/800 minicomputer. Throughout the rest of the chapter, this story illustrates the concepts of environmental ambiguity.

In 1978, Data General, the third largest minicomputer company in the world, was stung by industry leader Digital Equipment Corporation's (DEC) introduction of the VAX 11/780, the first 32-bit super-minicomputer. Although not surprised by the introduction, Data General was caught flat-footed. After several failed design projects, it did not have a competing machine and needed one badly.

During the mid-1970s, Data General split its engineering staff between two locations: the company headquarters in Westborough, Massachusetts, and a new facility in Research Triangle Park, North Carolina. The split had been very controversial. Many engineers refused to move their families to a new state and thus severely limited their careers. Not only had the department been split into two distant locations, but the work had been divided as well, with the Westborough group focused on maintaining and updating the older Eclipse line of computers while the new group worked on developing new designs for more exciting modern systems. Tom West headed up the Eclipse engineering group in Westborough that was designated to maintain the older systems.

Although the North Carolina team had been officially tasked with the job of designing Data General's first 32-bit super-mini, West wanted a shot at it too. Several times, he attempted to convince senior management to support the Eclipse group in creating an additional design, only to be shot down. Eventually, he came up with an interpretation of the environment that would prove compelling to both senior management and the engineers who would eventually work on the system that became known as the Eagle.

These are the key elements of his story:

- Data General needs a 32-bit super-mini to compete effectively with DEC.

- If the North Carolina design team fails again to complete a system, Data General will be in peril.

- The Eclipse group will continue to maintain the Eclipse systems and won't try to build new systems, which is the task of the North Carolina team.

- The Eclipse group will build a new 32-bit upgraded version of the current 16-bit Eclipse systems that remains backward-compatible with the older models.

- The 32-bit Eclipse will be Data General's insurance policy in case the North Carolina team fails.

The Foundation for Geekwork

As leaders and geeks together develop clarity about the setting in which their tripartite relationship takes place, that clarity serves as the intangible foundation on which geekwork is performed. In a building, the foundation supports critical physical infrastructure, such as columns, walls, floors, plumbing, and electrical systems, that holds the building together and makes it work. Environmental clarity serves a similar function with geekwork, but the critical systems here are supporting ideas. Since geekwork is carried out through thought and creativity, it requires intellectual and emotional infrastructure. In addition to environmental clarity, these supporting ideas are purpose, identity, and meaning, which collectively I call the foundation for geekwork (see Figure 9.3).

Defining Purpose

The first idea that relies on environmental clarity is organizational purpose, which is a clearly articulated reason for being that remains constant even as products, strategies, and organizational structures change. Without a clear picture of the environment, it would be nearly impossible to outline a meaningful purpose.

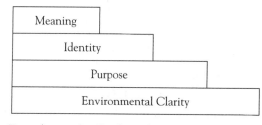

FIGURE 9.3. Foundation for Geekwork.

Not every organization has a purpose, but more should. Many of the most successful companies and groups have a purpose that offers their customers, employees, investors, partners, and suppliers clarity about what they do and why. Purpose offers a sense of continuity to the organization and contributes to developing collective identity and individual meaning. It also contributes to the resolution of environmental ambiguity by answering the fundamental question, "Why are we here beyond just making money?"

Don't confuse purpose with the other ideas that are commonly held up as the big conceptually supporting structures of an organization such as strategy, product, values, or goals. Each is different from purpose. Strategy is a long-term, high-level approach to the problems and markets that drives activity selection within a company. It may change as purpose stays constant. Products are just the collection of physical products and services that a company bundles together to meet the needs of a customer. They shift even more frequently than strategy does. And although they are an expression of a strategy, they are neither a strategy unto themselves nor a purpose. Values are the core principles that drive decision making. These can be just as stable as purpose, but they do not answer the question, "Why are we here?" Rather, they focus on the question, "How will we act while we are here?" Goals are measurable indicators of progress toward fulfilling purpose, but not a purpose in themselves. For example, if your organization's purpose is "to improve human life through the application of biotechnology," a goal may be "to bring an antimalaria drug to market by the end of the decade that can be easily afforded in Third World countries."

A well-defined purpose concentrates lots of information about an organization into a very short statement. By answering the question, "Why are we here?" many of the other fundamental questions of environmental ambiguity are answered by implication. Purpose communicates information on such other questions as, "Whom do we serve?" "What value we deliver?" and "What are our core values?"

> Tom West defined several purposes for Data General's Eagle project and emphasized different ones to different audiences. To the company's senior executives, he emphasized that the project was primarily an insurance policy against the failure of the North Carolina team. To the team members, his purpose took on a more urgent tone. To them, he expressed confidence that the North Carolina team would fail again and that the Eagle was the only hope for Data General's future success. For the team, the purpose of the Eagle was to save the company.

Establishing Identity

The ideas of organizational environment and purpose influence the development of the next important idea, identity. Both group and, to a lesser degree, individual identity provide essential support to geekwork.

Throughout life, each of us must grapple with issues of identification and self-concept. Although most intense during childhood and adolescence, self-definition does not end after high school. We constantly revise our own internalized image of ourselves as we grow, learn, and change throughout life. Self-concept provides us information about who we are, how we act, who others are, and how we expect to interact with them.

Without going too far into psychological theory, we can describe two distinct sources of identity: associations with groups of other individuals and internalized individual beliefs and values. You develop a sense of who you are through a combination of what you believe and whom you associate with.

Group Affiliation. The first influence on the sense of identity is group affiliation. These groups can be any collection of people, like professional associations, political parties, families, or community groups. Through these associations, you may identify yourself in many different ways simultaneously. For example, you may consider yourself to be a native Chicagoan, a Catholic, a Rotarian, a Cubs fan, a University of California Los Angeles alumnus or alumna, and an American citizen. Each association carries with it an image of members of that group that defines a standard set of characteristics with which you may identify. When you adopt some of the charac-teristics of the image of group members, you have modified your identity through the influence of affiliation.

In industrial and postindustrial societies, one's work identity becomes an important part of the pastiche that is postmodern adult self-identification. And so today, a geek may identify with a variety of groups in the work environment, including company, depart-ment, project team, and functional specialty, but may also identify with extraorganizational groups too, such as industry associations or groups only loosely defined by technical specialty or certification. The more important that work is in their lives, the more geeks build some of their own internal self-image by adopting characteristics from each of their work group affiliations.

On the Eagle project, the team members began to derive a sense of identity from association with the project. Huddled together in the dingy basement of corporate headquarters, the team members developed a strong sense of affiliation with the project in general and also with their subgroup. The team had been divided into two distinct groups that took on separate responsibilities, and they developed separate identities. Each group even got its own nickname. The "Hardy Boys," as they became known, designed the hardware for the new system. The "Micro Kids" spent their time writing the intricate software known as microcode.

Personal Values and Attitudes. The other influence on identity comes from internalized personalized values and attitudes. Values and attitudes represent the standards, patterns, or principles one applies to assessing the desirability of things, events, and people. We all have our personal opinions about what makes something desirable, and for each person, these patterns of evaluation tend to be relatively stable over time. In Chapter Two, we talked about some of the more common values and attitudes among geeks, such as the passion for reason, love for puzzles, and the importance of independence. These values and attitudes are complex combinations of emotions, experience, reason, and faith. Many of these find their beginnings in our family of origin, while others are experientially developed, adopted from group affiliations, or learned.

What's important about these values and attitudes is that each individual in the workplace uses a personal lens through which he or she views work and organization. Based on their understanding of the environment and the organization's purpose and culture, they evaluate the importance of their work, the desirability of the organization, and the nobility of its purpose. Each individual's values and attitudes influence whether that person finds meaning in their work.

Tom West recruited young engineers for his project, mostly fresh from college. He wanted junior people not yet tainted with the cynicism of office politics who were eager to build new systems. He felt it important that the engineers on the project have an undiminished passion for creation, as well as some naiveté about the ambitious scope of the technological and schedule goals for the project. So he selected team members based in part on their attitude toward creativity and the priority they placed on work.

Finding Meaning

The last of the supporting ideas is that of finding meaning in work. Some people look to their work to contribute meaning to their lives, and some don't. For some, punching the time clock and taking home a paycheck is all the meaning that they expect from work. They don't look to their work life to help give their lives significance.

That's a relatively rare attitude for geeks, especially for those who work on products. Geeks yearn for meaning. They spend most of their waking hours thinking about and manipulating symbols, and at some level, most want their work to symbolize more than just a paycheck. If they don't find meaning in their work, they will look for it elsewhere. At the same time, geeks don't want to talk openly about meaning or spirituality at work. But don't let that fool you. There is a craving for significance that geek leaders must acknowledge and fill without getting too touchy-feely.

Meaning develops through viewing the rest of the ideas in the foundation through the lens of individual values and attitudes. The more a person sees in those ideas that support and fulfill his or her desires and values, the more work will feel meaningful. For example, if one of your core values is that you enjoy serving others, then if your job includes client contact with appreciative users, you are more likely to find meaning in your work than if your job was solely to sit in a cubicle all day and code without ever contacting users.

Because meaning is a very individual reaction, leaders don't get direct control over how others evaluate the environment. They may be able to influence followers' interpretation of the workplace, but not their complex emotional responses to it. If geeks are to find meaning in work, it will be rooted in their views of the ideas in the foundation for geekwork.

It's difficult to say exactly what meaning each person on the Eagle project drew from their participation, but from Kidder's descriptions in *Soul of a New Machine* and subsequent press interviews, two themes seemed prominent. First, most team members felt that being part of the group that would save the company gave them a sense of importance; their work had significance. Second, they felt that successfully completing the project would earn them the right to do it again—to participate in the design of another completely new system, the ultimate reward for a geek.

How the Foundation Supports Geekwork

The ideas in the foundation provide conceptual and emotional support for the responsibilities of the geek leader. While environmental clarity and organizational purpose assist a leader's efforts to furnish external representation and provide internal coordination, the entire foundation becomes involved in supporting his attempts to nurture motivation (see Figure 9.4).

Supporting Internal Coordination

Internal coordination is supported by the two ideas in the foundation that geek leaders have the most direct influence on: environmental clarity and organizational purpose. You may recall from Chapter Seven that internal coordination carries two categories of responsibilities: establishing and maintaining the work environment and facilitating tasks. The foundation for geekwork supports leaders' ability to fill both needs.

In establishing and maintaining the work environment, a solid foundation helps an organization to be efficient and effective. First, let's look at effectiveness. Due to both the nature of geeks and the constraints of geekwork, most technology organizations need to make many decentralized decisions. The knowledge inversion where geeks know more about the details of their work than their leaders makes it difficult to centralize most decisions, and the independent nature of geeks makes it undesirable. But making effective

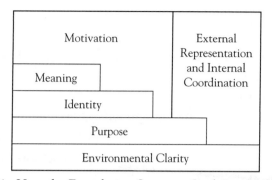

FIGURE 9.4. How the Foundation Supports Geek Leadership.

decisions in a decentralized environment is possible only when everyone involved has a clear understanding of the environment and the organization's purpose. The clarity and consistency of foundational information make it possible for disparate groups to apply similar priorities to their problems while also delivering more effective decisions that harness the creativity and insight of more people.

A well-managed foundation also serves to help leaders with conflict resolution. When problems arise between group members, a common understanding of the environment can become the basis on which issues are resolved. A good deal of conflict within project teams results from different interpretations of the environment and the best responses to it, so a common understanding of the conceptual foundation can help prevent and resolve conflicts.

A common understanding of the environment and organizational purpose also assists in making groups efficient. Due to time constraints on projects, most geekwork requires parallel work efforts. Project teams must work on many aspects of a problem simultaneously rather than tackle one thing at a time. But to keep everyone heading in the same direction while making reasonably coordinated decisions, each person needs that common understanding of environment and purpose. The assumptions and interpretations made in managing environmental ambiguity make it possible for geekwork to be done without a completely centralized management structure.

In facilitating tasks, the foundation is supportive in several ways. It can help to set meaningful goals that garner the commitment of geeks. Goals that aren't tied to a common understanding of the environment tend to be ignored. Those that have clear ties to external constraints or competition make more sense than just arbitrary targets. Many times I've seen executives set deadlines for projects that seem arbitrary to geeks, and so the geeks work at whatever pace they think appropriate, without regard for the deadline. When project teams understand the reasons for a time or budget goal, they are much more likely to work to meet it.

The foundation also helps with setting and communicating the priorities for resource allocation. In an organization where there is a shared understanding of environment and purpose, there are fewer questions about how priorities are being set, about why one project gets more people and money than another. The process is more transparent, and geeks generally feel that open decisions are more fair and easier to support, even if they don't like them.

> Tom West's environmental clarity was essential to the team's functioning and efficiency. Although the team had been split into two groups, the organization was relatively unstructured. Within the subgroups, individuals took on responsibilities almost organically, without direction, just because they knew specific things had to be done. What guided them in taking on individual responsibility was not directives from above that tasks should be completed, but the team's recognition that they had to do these things in order to meet the constraints and goals that were given to them. Without a clear understanding of the environment, team members would have been completely reliant on managers for task specifications.

Supporting External Representation

The ideas of the foundation support a geek leader's efforts in external representation in four key areas: aligning business with technology, acquiring resources, managing client expectations, and recruiting.

Perhaps most important, environmental clarity and purpose provide a clear conceptual basis for discussions about aligning technology with business. Without a clearly articulated interpretation of the environment, it would be very difficult to hold discussions with peers, superiors, and external partners. A leader would be part of discussions without a clear worldview or agenda to pursue.

Similarly, a clearly articulated purpose also becomes critical for a leader engaged in negotiating to acquire organizational resources. It is very difficult to make compelling cases for technology and staffing investments without a clear vision of how they would benefit and relate to the priorities of the rest of the organization.

Environmental clarity and organizational purpose also serve as a framework for managing client expectations. As projects progress, it often becomes necessary to make trade-offs between the business functions and technical scope of a product in order to bring the project to completion. Setting priorities in a consistent manner and gaining the consent of clients is much easier when you can deliver a compelling argument grounded in a complete picture of the environment. It can help to diffuse arguments over budgets, placing the discussions in a broader context of the good of the whole organization.

A well-managed foundation can also be used to help attract new geeks into the company. Since the ideas have already been developed to be compelling for geeks, the same ideas should prove attractive when recruiting outsiders.

Tom West found that environmental clarity and purpose were absolutely critical to the Eagle project. In fact, until he was able to supply them, the project could not occur. While his story was less than compelling, senior management rejected his proposals. Not until he came up with a more compelling interpretation of reality did they finally relent and fund the project.

Supporting Motivation

Finally, all the ideas of the foundation support a leader's efforts to nurture motivation. You cannot directly motivate geeks, but you can try to create the conditions under which they motivate themselves.

Environmental clarity and organizational purpose support motivation by enabling geeks to work more independently. With a solid understanding of the environment, they are able to make their own decisions about day-to-day matters without having to check with the boss constantly. For geeks, who generally have a strong independent streak, autonomy fosters motivation.

Environmental clarity also creates the opportunity for engendering external competition. Targeting an external enemy both creates unity within groups and harnesses the machismo and competitive drive of geeks. Identifying the enemy is part of interpreting the environment.

All of the ideas of the foundation are critical in finding the meaning in work, which is one of the most important sources of intrinsic motivation. The dedication and commitment that come from doing work with a purpose higher than just delivering a paycheck is one of the most potent influences on the energy, enthusiasm, and drive with which geeks engage with their work. Without a solid foundation, meaning can be derived only from personal values and goals separate from the organization's. Without context, geeks are motivated by self-centered purposes.

The Eagle project team members were clearly motivated. Most practically gave up the rest of their lives for more than a year while the project progressed. So many voluntarily worked nights and weekends that eventually West had to make a rule that everyone was required to take Sundays off, fearing that the entire group would burn out.

This level of motivation and engagement resulted from the support of the foundation that he had built. Each individual viewed the ideas of the foundation through personal values to find meaning and motivation. For some, the mission of saving the company proved compelling. For others, the interesting nature of the work was reward enough. The sense of camaraderie that developed within the group contributed to their motivation, but for many, and especially for West, the sense of competition with the North Carolina team also proved critical.

So how did the Eagle project turn out? After more than a year of grueling work, the group managed to deliver the machine. The North Carolina team did eventually deliver its system, but not until much later than the Eagle. West's machine debuted in the spring of 1980 and sold well for several years. Unfortunately, Data General was not prepared for the personal computer revolution, and the company began a long decline.

Tips for Managing Environmental Ambiguity

Here are some thoughts about what you as a geek leader need to do to ensure that your group develops a solid foundation for geekwork:

• *Don't assume that geeks understand the environment.* Many leaders assume that because geeks are smart, they have the same ideas about the environment as business leaders do. Usually it's not so. Generally, geeks expend most of their mental energy on technology rather than business.
• *Don't assume that geeks don't care about the environment.* Too many leaders assume that because geeks spend so much energy on technology, they don't care about other things. Often they do care, but just don't find environmental issues as engaging as the technical ones.
• *Discuss and debate interpretations of the environment openly.* Leaders need to initiate conversations with geeks about the outside

world, both to monitor what geeks know and think and to engage them in developing clarity.

• *Frame technical issues in business terms*. Use discussions about technical issues to link technology and business. The more often you can link them up, the better geeks will understand the direct connections between their technical world and the external environment.

Summary

FUNDAMENTAL QUESTIONS

• What is ambiguity, and why is it important to geek leaders?

• What types of ambiguity must be managed?

• Why do geeks need to know so much about their environment?

KEY IDEAS

• The most important and subtle role of a geek leader is managing ambiguity.

• Ambiguity occurs within geek organizations at three levels described by the Hierarchy of Ambiguity model: environmental, structural, and task.

• Environmental ambiguity encompasses the big-picture questions behind all geekwork, including issues of identity, purpose, and meaning.

• Resolving environmental ambiguity helps provide a foundation of ideas on which individual and collective motivation can form.

• The key ideas of the foundation for geekwork are environmental clarity, organizational purpose, individual and group identity, and meaning.

10

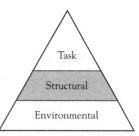

Selecting and Organizing Geekwork

The second level of ambiguity that geek leaders manage is structural ambiguity, which relates to selecting and organizing geekwork. Using the assumptions and interpretations that result from managing environmental ambiguity, geek leaders guide the selection of business and technological goals and the organization of geeks to pursue them. For technical groups, structural ambiguity encompasses two deceptively simple questions:

- What are we going to do?
- How are we going to do it?

The deceptively simple answers to these questions are, respectively, "projects" and "processes." Work is selected and usually organized into projects. Projects are then structured using processes that help determine the organizational design, selection, and sequencing of tasks and the management of risk.

Projects

As a consultant who specializes in the management of geek groups, I get to see almost every method that humans have conceived for organizing work. It fascinates me endlessly to see the benefits and dysfunctions of the various choices, but all my travels have convinced me that projects are the optimal format for geekwork.

There is a certain irony in this. The project form of work is almost as old as humanity itself. Once communication advanced to the point of allowing cooperation and coordination, groups of early people must have banded together to hunt large game, build shelters, and migrate from one place to another. And today, after evolving through many methods of organizing work, from early agrarian family farms to large Roman slaveholding agricultural estates, from the medieval craft and textile industries to the modern factory, ultramodern, intellect-driven, knowledge-intensive geekwork roots itself in the project.

What is it that makes projects such a productive approach to geekwork? There is a special interaction that takes place—a synergy among geek personalities, the character of geekwork, and the nature of projects that makes them ideally suited to one another. It would be hard to imagine a more potent mix of mutually supportive people and processes.

The Nature of Projects

Both subtle and complex, the project organization of work continues to be one of the most common and unstudied methods of work. Although most of us talk about projects and project management every day, *project* has become a loosely defined phrase used to refer to almost any sort of work.

If you want to optimize geekwork, it's important to think carefully about projects—to examine their effects and understand the differences between true projects and other forms of work that may not provide the same benefits. Then you must build an organization designed to support projects rather than simply tolerate them.

What Projects Are. The first and easiest way to consider what projects are is to look around for the evidence that they leave behind—the artifacts that are the ultimate result. Wherever there is a bridge, there was a project. If you see a building, there was a project. The street in front of your home resulted from a project, and so did your home. As a tourist, you might visit other project artifacts, like the Eiffel Tower, the Coliseum in Rome, the pyramids in Egypt, or the Sears Tower in Chicago. Neil Armstrong's first footprint on the moon was the culmination of a massive project. On the Web, you might surf over to Amazon.com, ebay.com, or Yahoo.com. Every thirty-second television advertisement and half-hour sitcom episode resulted from a project. And the words that you are now reading are the end product of a project.

Although there are many different types of projects, they all share a number of common characteristics:

- *Unique output.* The most prominent feature of a project is that its output is unique. Whether the outcome of the project is a physical artifact or an intangible service, no other project will produce the exact same thing. Although projects may share similar processes and approaches, each project's output will reflect the personalities of the participants, the quality and timing of available resources, and political and other environmental forces that acted on the project team. Collectively, these factors ensure that no two projects ever have exactly the same result.
- *Specific goals.* Projects are initiated to resolve particular problems or exploit specific opportunities. Few projects receive support and funding without explicitly stated goals and intended outcomes. Most projects aim to boost profitability, improve competitiveness, enable services, or alleviate political pressure. Geeks love the project form of work at least in part because it appeals to their problem-solution model of thinking.
- *Professional judgment.* Projects are never simple. Given a specific set of objectives, there may be myriad ways of achieving them—of matching project actions and artifacts with goals. The selection of appropriate means always requires the application of professional judgment. Although some detailed project methodologies attempt to standardize output and minimize the influence of

professional judgment, the results of all projects reflect the quality and creativity of individual decisions made by specialized experts.

• *Distinctive events*. Every project is a one-time event. Even with the same personnel and identical goals, no two projects will progress in the same manner. Just as when two baseball teams meet with the same players and on the same field but on different days, the outcome of a game will be subject to many other factors. Projects are more than their output. They are experiences and performances that deliver results.

• *Change focus*. Ultimately, the intention of every project is to effect change of some sort. Projects are rarely initiated to maintain the status quo. They include some element of change to a product, a community, a process, or an element of infrastructure. This is why their outputs and events are unique.

• *Time boundaries*. Projects are ephemeral, time-bounded events ending in one of three ways: mission accomplished, mission aborted, or canceled due to failure to meet goals. Any work that does not have a clearly defined end point is not a project but represents some other form of production.

• *Temporary resources*. Most projects require the expertise and effort of many people, assembling skills and labor into temporary groups capable of accomplishing the project goals. Some professionals may be assigned to a project for its duration, while others may be present for peak periods of work and still others may only advise or supervise intermittently.

• *Distinct and interdependent activities*. Projects are composed of activities, most of them unique and nonrepetitive. These activities are usually interrelated to one another in such a way that one or more tasks must be completed, or at least partially completed, to allow other tasks to progress. For example, if you are trying to design and deploy a small set of networked computers in an office, you can't order the equipment until the design is done and you know the right equipment to acquire.

• *Completion focus*. Although project goals are as varied as human imagination, every project shares one: to finish. This should be the one unifying goal for all members of a project team, whether minor contributor or responsible manager. This casts an especially unusual role for project managers. While most managers focus on optimizing and maintaining long-term operations, project managers should attempt to work themselves out of a job, making their positions obsolete.

- *Conscious constitution.* All projects are formed through an active decision. As one-time unique events, they cannot be initiated through managerial inaction. Someone in a position of authority must take explicit action to begin an effort.

What Projects Are Not. Why is it so important to distinguish between projects and other forms of work? Many times, groups think that they are doing projects, or started out with one, only to change their approach and lose the benefits that projects confer.

One of my clients, let's call it WidgetWare, had several software products that had been shipping in ever-changing versions to customers for more than fifteen years. Each product had one software developer who was responsible for maintaining and improving that product. When clients would call in to complain about some feature or ask for some new functionality, the developer would decide whether and when to modify the product. Each of these requested changes was referred to as "a project" for the developer, who would be working on ten to twenty "projects" at a time. As the developer tried to manage each project as a separate entity, things became very confused. Priorities became muddied. Accounting for time became impossible. The code for each product became a tangled mess, since the developer never attempted to truly design a coherent block of changes as a single software release. In short, these developers weren't really doing projects. They had created small departments that constantly worked on a treadmill without beginning or end. This was difficult for the staff to deal with, hard on existing customers, who never knew what to expect, and limited new product sales since salespeople never knew exactly what they were selling.

All of this happened because the development group wasn't clear on the concept of a project. Here are a few ways to organize work that are often confused with projects:

- *Departments*. It's easy to think that because a group of people work together on similar things within a company that they are doing projects, but it isn't necessarily so. Departments are enduring organizational structures, created to fill ongoing operational needs. Departments tend to focus on a functional area, such as product development, manufacturing, or accounting. Although they may undertake projects by temporarily assigning subgroups of people to fill some one-time need, usually they spawn subdepartments that take on the departmental nature of their parent groups and become long-term entities that endure beyond their original mission.

- *Teams*. A team of people working together may or may not form a project team. In the workplace the word *team* is often used to refer to any group of people working together. Organizational behavior professors have a much more restricted definition, and groups commonly called teams don't fit this stricter sense of the word. Groups colloquially called teams are not necessarily time bounded. They may be departments or subdepartments with ongoing missions or may constantly struggle to justify their existence. Teams may not share interdependent activities. Instead, they may be a work-sharing group: the members are not interdependent, but each is performing essentially the same work, combining their efforts to balance the workload.

- *Committees*. Cross-functional committees are often confused with project teams. These groups tend to be brought into being to provide long-term coordination on some specific topic between disparate departments engaged in ongoing operations. Although they may have a unifying goal, it is usually not one that conforms to the problem-solution model that centers on projects. Committees tend to become part of the human infrastructure of an organization rather than disbanding since the issues that they address cannot be completely resolved.

- *Outsourced individuals or groups.* Although groups of people may be contracted to deliver a particular project, don't confuse the legal form of the employment relationship with the way that the work itself is organized. Too often, a consulting or outsourcing company will use the word *project* interchangeably with the word *contract.* They are not synonymous. The contract between the hiring company and the consultant represents only the legal form of the contractual relationship.

Projects as Theater. To think of projects only as a way to organize tasks and people is to miss many of the reasons that they are so central to geekwork. Much of the power of projects to drive geekwork does not directly derive from its organizational form; it comes from its narrative structure. You can think of projects as a form of theater played out in the workplace every day. And as in a play, assumptions about relationships between actors, audience, script, costume, lighting, scenery, and story serve as a backdrop against which roles, actions, themes, motivations, and meanings are defined.

Do you ever wonder why so many famous film and television actors choose to work in small theater productions? Clearly, it's not for the money. It's primarily because live theater offers a fulfilling experience of narrative that work in other media cannot. In film, scenes are shot repeatedly and out of sequence, reducing the actor's experience of narrative to a series of brief episodes. In contrast, theater offers a complete experience in which the entire story is played out and viewed simultaneously, in which the actors and audience travel together through the narrative as the play unfolds. Theater offers immediacy and coherence missing from other types of acting work.

For participants, the experience of being part of a project is much like that of being an actor in a play. Projects too offer immediacy, urgency, and coherence that other forms of work lack. They bring together all of the elements of performance that give shape and meaning to what otherwise may be only a series of disjointed tasks.

Why Projectize?

In many organizations, projects are still the exception rather than the rule when organizing work within the technical department. So why should you as a leader consider putting all the effort into transforming day-to-day work into projects? Why should you put the effort into monitoring whether projects continue to be projects or slip into other sorts of work?

There are number of reasons that projects turn out to be so central to the execution of geekwork. Projects provide benefits that are tangible, concrete, immediate paybacks for the effort it takes to organize them. Individually, these reasons are good motivators, but collectively they make projects indispensable to geekwork. Projects offer the following advantages:

• *Aid alignment.* During their initial phases, well-managed projects attempt to state their goals, outputs, and methods for production explicitly. The process of forging these statements provides a forum in which the needs of the business and the outputs of a project are balanced.

• *Enhance motivation.* Projects are ideally suited to enhancing geek motivation. Many of their features fit perfectly with geek personalities. For instance, creating unique outputs engages the creativity and curiosity of geeks. Using their professional judgment appeals to their independent nature, and the fact that no two projects are alike prevents boredom.

• *Ensure that you do only important stuff.* Because projects require conscious constitution, they occur only when the goals of a project prove important to an organization. In many alternative work structures, active management decisions need not be made before work begins. Departments, teams, or committees are often able to begin work without first obtaining the consent of those affected, creating organizational inertia behind investments of questionable value.

• *Delineate endings.* While projects are designed to end, most other forms of organizational structure are intended to endure and self-propagate rather than disband. And without well-defined endings, work loses its narrative structure that provides so much of the motivating force and meaning that teams need.

• *Limit scope*. Projects force you to choose the size of the problem you want to address, limiting the amount of work that gets done at one time. It should be obvious that limited expectations are much more likely to be satisfied than limitless ones. One of the great hazards of projects is allowing them to expand beyond their original mission to include work outside the initial scope of the project, a phenomenon commonly referred to as "scope creep."

• *Build client relationships*. Because projects require conscious constitution, they also require explicit sponsorship. That is, every project needs a client—someone who takes final responsibility for the willingness to pay the bill. Some people treat this necessity as a burden, but they should treat it as a benefit. Projects without sponsors rarely deliver the value they aspire to.

• *Compel client focus*. Because true projects require clients from the outset, project teams feel much more compelled to pay attention to and attempt to fill the needs of their clients. The implication is not that people in other organizational structures are less concerned about their clients; rather, they may be simply less aware of them due to the decoupling effect of permanent organizational structures.

• *Force out deadwood*. Project teams are much less tolerant of noncontributing members than are people engaged in other forms of work organization. When a team believes in its goals, is truly focused on completion, and believes that deadlines are real, participants have few excuses for allowing limited project resources to be squandered on poor performers. The foxhole-type loyalty that team members develop for each other prevents them from allowing their comrades to become victims of incompetent or incapable coworkers.

• *Force trade-offs*. Because projects are limited by time and resources, their constraints demand creativity if project teams are to fulfill the goals of the project while honoring the limitations. Although geeks may grumble and complain, these limits provide

good puzzles to challenge the imagination and ingenuity of a project team.

Processes

Once you have answered the question, "What will we do?" you've
got to answer the other question of structural ambiguity: "How will
we do it?" The answer is that you will follow some form of process,
which will answer the more detailed questions:

- How will the project team be organized?
- What tasks will be done, and in what sequence?
- How will the inherent risks of technical projects be explicitly
  managed?

These questions must be effectively answered for all projects,
whether they are small with only one person working for only a day
or hundreds of people working for years.

These are the questions that are addressed by what geeks call
methodology. Over the history of IT, a number of systems development, deployment, and maintenance methodologies have been created in an attempt to render technical projects more predictable.
Almost every consulting firm has a proprietary variant that it touts
as insurance that its projects have better outcomes than anyone
else's. These methodologies range from extraordinarily detailed,
step-by-step approaches meant to cover every conceivable situation
to new "light" methodologies that have been gaining ground over
recent years. The detailed ones attempt to prescribe every activity
that must take place in what sequence in order to finish a project.
The "light" methodologies are more like a general set of good ideas
about how to approach projects.

In my experience, none of these approaches has proved perfect
for every situation, but the one thing that most of them have in
common is that they are all ignored. Although most projects start
out with good intentions about following one methodology or

another, very few follow them through to completion. Under the pressure of project constraints, they descend into chaotic, intuitively scheduled activities.

I will not devote too much space here to these important project management issues since they fall outside the scope of this book. My goal in addressing them is just to outline at a high level the issues involved and to make it easier to understand the choices that must be made in order to deliver a technical project successfully. (For more information about project management, see some of my favorite books listed in the References.)

Team Structure

To answer the first detailed question, "How will the project team be organized?" there are only two basic strategies: classic hierarchical management or self-managed team of peers, each with strengths and weaknesses. These two can be combined in many complex and imaginative ways, but at core there are only two basic strategies.

Hierarchical Teams. The traditional approach to management is top down: one person is designated responsible for the project, with the authority to make decisions. Everyone else on the project team then reports either directly or indirectly to that person. Typically, that person is called the project or program manager.

The hierarchical structure has endured for many reasons. First, it's comfortable for both managers and workers since it is so familiar. Managers like the sense of control and power that comes from being on top of others. Subordinates often like the model because it provides clear lines of authority and control. Theoretically, they need to please only one boss to do well at a company. There's no confusion. For many people, there simply is no other way to think about organizing people, and they rebel against the idea that other structures are possible.

Over the past twenty years, many limitations of this type of organization have come to the light, especially for those engaged in the creation and distribution of knowledge-intensive intellectual property—for example:

- *High communications overhead.* Given so many layers of management, the amount of communication necessary to keep everyone involved in a project informed about status and changes often becomes overwhelming.
- *Communications breakdowns.* Because the project manager becomes a central hub for communications and decisions within a project, he can become easily overwhelmed with incoming information and requests for attention. The success of a project is very sensitive to the personal communications, organizational, and technical skills of the central project manager.
- *Fragile project structure.* Because the project manager serves as the information hub and perhaps even the technical visionary behind the project, should this person decide to leave the organization or become incapacitated during the project, much of the project knowledge goes with that person. Some projects never recover from the loss of a project manager.
- *Poor decision making.* In the pure theoretical hierarchical model, the project manager is the central decision maker, retaining all authority. Too often, project managers feel that they must or should demonstrate their power by making judgments on their own. This engages the creativity, experience, expertise, and wisdom of only one person rather than harnessing the neurons of everyone on the project.

Even with these and other serious limitations, the hierarchical team remains by far the more common structure. Relatively few leaders have felt willing to take the perceived risk of trying something less traditional.

Self-Managed Teams. Since the early 1970s, experiments have been taking place with new organizational designs that seek to address the issues that face hierarchical teams. Most fall under the category of the self-managed team—one managed collectively by the team members themselves rather than by a single designated manager, as in the hierarchical model. This shared management is usually distributed over a core group of people who are collectively delegated authority over the project and are held responsible for its success. Decisions are made by all the team members rather than by a single all-powerful manager.

Typically, the team is not made up of undifferentiated people assigned to the project. Each member of the core team is assigned responsibility for one functional specialty or some aspect of success for the project. In some environments, these are called cross-functional teams. For example, in a typical software development project, one core team member will be responsible for development, another for client advocacy, another for project management, and so forth. In assigning individuals to represent the interests of a particular specialty, a balance of power is created within the core team, and negotiations must take place about how best to meet the project's goals.

This approach offers many advantages but some disadvantages for geekwork. It addresses effectively many failures and bottlenecks of communications in the hierarchical model. There is no single point of failure in the communications chain, since there is no single project manager. Similarly, by design, it engages the creativity of all members of the team in resolving the project problems rather than relying solely on the abilities of a single project manager. In addition, the productivity of these types of teams tends to be greater than that of traditional teams.

But there are some downsides as well. Both managers and participants often find their first experiences with this approach disorienting. The way these teams work challenges many of their core assumptions about the work environment. For example, many teams and managers at first are uncomfortable with the idea that no one person is in charge of the group. "Someone's got to be in charge," they often say. "Someone's got to take responsibility for the project." But in fact, these are assumptions that have proven to be untrue. Especially with geekwork, once teams become used to working without a boss, they often become more productive than they were before.

Some companies have begun to use these types of teams regularly for software and hardware development and deployment. For example, Microsoft has developed its own version of the self-managed team approach, which has been incorporated in its own methodology known as the Microsoft Solutions Framework.

Task Process

The second detailed question about the project structure is, "What tasks should be done, and in what sequence?" Although it may seem an odd question to a nontechnical person, there is not any one clear answer to this question. There is no obviously right way to approach a technical problem. Despite almost half a century of experience with information technology, there still is no commonly agreed approach to task definition.

As with the team models, there are two basic families of approaches to project tasks: the waterfall model and the spiral model. Each has its strengths and weaknesses, and they can be hybridized when necessary.

Waterfall Task Processes. The waterfall approach is named for its representation on a project task chart called a Gantt chart, on which it looks like a downward-flowing staircase over which water might tumble. A waterfall project plan has these characteristics:

- *Phases.* A project is composed of a series of distinct phases.

- *Milestones.* Each phase concludes with a milestone.

- *Deliverables.* Milestones usually represent the delivery of some physical artifact, such as a document or a program, often referred to as a deliverable.

- *Unidirectionality.* Once each phase is finished and its milestone achieved, it is not repeated or revisited.

The waterfall approach represents the task process analogue of the hierarchical team. It is the classic of the industry. Even today, most projects are planned in this fashion.

It has many advantages. It is conceptually clear and so is easy to communicate to clients and project team members. Milestones are also good checkpoints at which the health of the project can be measured and plans adjusted. The distinct phase approach is good for complex projects, since complete analysis and design should be finished before construction begins.

It also has many serious disadvantages. The process is very slow. Phases must wait for the completion of their predecessors when it may be possible to continue based on provisional information. Because the process is so slow, there is a high likelihood of customer needs' changing as the project progresses. And the process is very inflexible and hard to use in the intense and time-driven market-place.

Perhaps its most important disadvantage is that few projects really run this way. It's just not realistic. In all my years in technology consulting, most projects I've seen are planned this way, but none of them actually progresses according to this sort of plan. Phases are always revisited and repeated. Documents are never signed off. No one can afford to wait until every last bit of information is negotiated in one phase before beginning the next. And you can't really freeze the business requirements months, if not years, in advance of delivery. Things change, and the products that projects build must too. Creativity doesn't work by plan, and inspiration knows no schedule.

Spiral Task Processes. The spiral approach, also sometimes called rapid application development, appeared in the 1980s and has been in use since then. Instead of emphasizing discrete phases and orderly conceptual progression, the spiral process is designed to couple client needs and project outputs tightly.

The spiral model is named for its iterative nature. It has these characteristics:

- *Prototypes.* The approach rapidly develops partial, nonfunctional sample systems that can be easily refined.
- *Client feedback.* The prototypes are shown to clients early and often to solicit feedback and ensure that their needs are being met.
- *Rapid cycles.* The time intervals between client feedback and integration of the feedback into prototypes can sometimes be measured in hours or days rather than weeks, months, or years, as in the waterfall approach.
- *Flexibility.* The approach is designed to be highly responsive to changes in the business climate.

Clearly this approach has some distinct advantages. It integrates clients well into the process, and the product is more likely to meet their needs. The focus on fast delivery helps build strong client relationships. And the process is very flexible.

It also has some serious problems. It is very difficult to use for technically complex projects, since it does not allow sufficient time or requirements stability for the design, construction, and testing of complex, hidden back-end architectures. Maintaining control of the scope of a project run this way can be difficult. It is also hard to know when to stop cycling and finish the project; there are no clear end points. It's also hard to monitor the health of these projects since there are no milestones with clearly complete parts of the project. Sometimes these types of projects seem to cycle forever.

Risk Management

The final question related to structural ambiguity, "How will the inherent risks of technical projects be explicitly managed?" is the one most often overlooked by technical teams. Everyone knows that technical projects are risky ventures: most fail to meet all of their objectives, and many fail to meet any of them. But few projects do explicit risk management.

Team structures and task processes are designed to help resolve the inherent ambiguity of technical projects. But no matter how detailed your plans or how well conceived your organizational structure, reality is always messier than whatever you planned for. These tools are designed to reduce ambiguity as much as possible. The more planning you do, the more you feel that you've conquered ambiguity.

In contrast, risk management is designed to acknowledge projects' inherent ambiguity and account for the variability of reality. Risk management is designed not to plan for what you know needs to be done but to plan for things that might happen that will derail your other plans.

In its simplest form, risk management consists of identifying things that might go wrong, their implications for the project, and how you can reduce the project's exposure to those events. For example, imagine that you are planning a rollout of one hundred desktop computers for a new office. There are many risks that might derail the schedule: some of the computers might not arrive on time, for example, or the power outlets in the new office might not be in the places indicated in the floor plan, making it impossible to plug in the systems as planned. The trick is to identify the most important risks and make plans to ensure that they don't derail the project should they occur.

Exactly how risk management is done is not as important as the fact that it is being done on projects. It may be the biggest return on investment you can get in project management.

Tips for Managing Structural Ambiguity

Here are a few suggestions for how to manage structural ambiguity effectively:

• *Clearly articulate goals for every project.* It's easy to assume that once you've decided to do a project, it must be obvious to everyone involved why it's being done. Unfortunately, that's not so. In fact, until you try to articulate the goals of a project for yourself, *you* may not even know. It's important to clarify the business, technical, and organizational goals for every project at the outset.

• *Make assumptions explicit.* Articulate the assumptions you have made about the business, technology, people, and process for a project. Too often, projects carry on long after their foundational assumptions are violated, only to find at the end that their reasons for being are no longer valid.

• *Avoid process extremes.* Most organizations that I work with fall into one of two categories: those that are relatively chaotic and have no commonly observed processes and those that have excessively rigid processes that are not adapted to specific projects. Neither extreme seems to serve geeks or their organizations well. Remember that process is a means to an end, not an end in itself.

Summary

FUNDAMENTAL QUESTIONS

• What is the importance of managing structural ambiguity?

• What are projects, and why is it important to organize work this way?

• What are the components of process, and how are they managed?

KEY IDEAS

• Geek leaders manage structural ambiguity by answering two key questions: What are we going to do? and How are we going to do it?

• Geekwork is selected and is most productively organized into projects.

• Once defined, projects require clear processes that describe team structure, task process, and risk management.

11

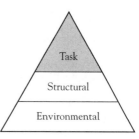

Uniting Geeks and Geekwork

The final level of ambiguity that geek leaders manage is task ambiguity. While structural ambiguity involves issues related to the selection and organization of geekwork, task ambiguity involves explicitly linking individual geeks to geekwork, that is, actually getting things done. Task ambiguity encompasses three key questions related to individual and small group productivity:

- Who are the characters in the story of a project?
- Who plays each role?
- What are the prerogatives of a geek leader, and how are they exercised?

To answer these questions, geek leaders use the selections and assumptions made in managing structural ambiguity to design project roles, assign individual geeks to fill those roles, and make judgments about products and performance.

Designing Project Roles

Geek leaders answer the first question of task ambiguity, "Who are the characters in the story of our project?" by defining project roles. Project roles are often mistaken for a box on an organization chart that describes the hierarchical position of a person in the pecking order of a project. Although an organization chart can help define one facet of a role, it is far from a comprehensive description. In fact, a project role is also not the same thing as the job of one particular person assigned to a project, since a single person may perform more than one role and more than one person may be assigned to the same role. A project role is also not the same as a job description, since it is much more than a list of tasks and expectations.

A project role is like a role in a play that does not yet have a cast, like the role of Hamlet in the Shakespeare play. The Hamlet on the page is the role of Hamlet, the archetypal Hamlet that then may be later inhabited by various actors. A project role is like a phantom project participant in a phantom project. It provides a comprehensive archetype of a project participant that includes information about the various facets:

- Individual goals—the purpose that the role serves and what it seeks to accomplish
- Relationship to overall goals—how the individual goals support and contribute to the attainment of the overall project goals
- Expected behavior—the manner in which one takes actions and interacts with others
- Artifacts—general information about the types of product that the role produces
- Tasks—the types of actions expected to support the project and produce the necessary artifacts
- Technical skills—the technical skills possessed by the role
- Nontechnical skills—the nontechnical soft skills possessed by the role

Project roles offer geeks a great deal more than just a dry job description or a generic task list. They offer a comforting coherence that gives shape and meaning to their tasks, a sense of social order and project structure that an organization chart can only hint at, and well-defined goals to which they can apply their expertise. In short, roles help geeks make sense of their work: the collective goals, the organizational environment, and their own part in a project. Geeks love project roles because they bring clarity to task ambiguity without imposing micromanagement from above. Project roles offer direction without arousing the resistance to control that geeks commonly feel.

Structuring Project Roles

Designing all the roles for a project is like completing the cast of characters for a play that you haven't written yet. You have named all the characters and described their behavioral characteristics, unique motivations, and histories that brought them to the play, but they don't yet have lines, scenes, acts, settings, or costumes. Technology projects are more like improvisation: once you have identified the characters, they will largely write the play for you.

But since the characters get to write the play, a geek leader must structure the roles carefully to ensure that the story concludes in a predictable and productive manner. There are five criteria for determining whether a set of project roles has been well defined:

- Task coverage, competence, and compatibility
- Clear and coherent goals
- Behavioral uniformity
- Constituent representation
- Advocacy system balance

When the project roles do not meet one or more of these criteria, it is unlikely that the project will finish optimally. It may not be a guarantee that a project will be a disaster, but it will be less than optimal.

Task Coverage, Competence, and Compatibility. The first criterion is really three in one. It gauges whether the roles embody task
coverage, competence, and compatibility. Task coverage ensures that
when the project roles are taken collectively, all the necessary tasks
are going to get done. If there are critical gaps in the range of
tasks that the roles will collectively fill, then things will fall through
the cracks, and the overall project will suffer.

Task competence ensures that the skills required to fill each role
are likely to be found in a single human being. You may define a
role where one person needs deep understanding of both quantum
mechanics and botany, but there aren't too many real people who
could fill that role. The knowledge and skill requirements for the
roles must be reasonable.

Task compatibility ensures that the combination of tasks envi-
sioned for a single person is possible to do at the same time. A role
may fulfill the task competence criterion in that a single person may
have the combination of skills required, but the tasks themselves
may not be plausible to do simultaneously on the same project. For
example, a single person may be a very capable programmer and a
good project manager, but doing both at the same time would be
quite difficult. The programming task requires long periods of deep
concentration without interruption, and the project manager tasks
require constant availability for communication. For project managers, interruptions are a normal and necessary part of the job. To
try to be both a programmer and a project manager simultaneously
would violate the task compatibility criterion.

Clear and Coherent Goals. The second criterion is that each role
must have clear and coherent goals that are explicitly articulated.
Goals focus roles. Without them, geeks end up unfocused, vacillat-
ing between competing priorities and trying to balance all the project variables themselves. With a single clear goal, it's much easier
to pursue a role vigorously.

Goals need to be associated with the overall success of a project and not task based. For example, ensuring customer satisfac-

tion is a well-defined goal; performing programming is not (it is a task).

If a role is assigned multiple goals, one must be set as the primary and others as subsidiary. No one can pursue two or more first priorities. One must take precedence over others. You can't reasonably expect one person to try to satisfy the client and minimize costs at the same time, for example. It's best to give these two conflicting goals to different people on the project and allow the advocacy system (described below) to balance them.

Behavioral Uniformity. The third criterion is that each role must reflect behavioral uniformity. Individual roles can be designed to require broad ranges of behaviors to complete all the tasks satisfactorily, but people have personalities and patterns of behaviors that they naturally exhibit. Just as it may be impossible to find a single person with disparate skills to fill an inappropriately defined role, it also may be difficult to find a person who can reasonably fulfill all the behavioral requirements as well. If a single role expects too broad a range of behaviors, no one will be able to do it well. For example, the role of a system tester requires someone who is very patient and attentive to detail. Good testers tend to be introverted and precise. Client advocates need to be extroverted and communicative to synchronize expectations. It would be very hard to find one person to fill a role requiring both introverted and extroverted behavior.

Constituent Representation. The fourth criterion is constituent representation. Because most technical projects need to balance the competing interests of many constituencies, each needs to have its interests explicitly represented in the project team. The goals of individual roles need to be aligned with the interests of a single interest group. That way, as project decisions are made and trade-offs negotiated, none of the important stakeholders will be without representation. When constituent representation is combined with a balanced advocacy system, projects will align with the business almost automatically, resolving their own ambiguity and making good decisions as they go.

Advocacy System Balance. The final criterion is advocacy system balance. In a sense, you can look at a project team as a legislative body like the U.S. Senate. In the Senate, each state elects two senators to advocate for their particular needs and desires. Collectively, the senators form a single body that attempts to balance the needs of all states through an advocacy system that requires them to come to some form of consensus in order to act. In theory, the compromises that are worked out through the advocacy system should be as well aligned with the needs of the states as possible. The balance of power created by the organizational structure of the Senate provides a crucible in which advocacy may be channeled into productive conflict that results in optimal, if not perfect, decisions for the nation.

In technical projects, you can think of project roles as senatorial positions, each with a perspective to advocate. The structure of the project organization (for example, a hierarchical team or a self-managed team) serves much like the rules of the Senate, providing the vessel in which balance of power may be channeled into productive conflict resulting in decisions for the project. If the power between the roles is balanced, it ensures that the roles will work out optimal, if not perfect, project decisions that best reflect the balanced needs of all the various constituencies. If the advocacy system is unbalanced, the group represented by the excessively powerful role will have its interests disproportionately reflected in project decisions.

One project on which I worked demonstrates the effects of imbalance. We were developing a new software system that would help manage fast food restaurants. The executive sponsoring the project decided that the software development manager should be in charge of the entire project. This manager had absolutely no experience running a restaurant yet decided that he knew exactly what the clients needed and refused to listen to anyone else's opinion on how the system should work. The system ended up looking like a programmer's system rather than a restaurant manager's system. The screens were designed to reflect the internal structure of the code rather than the way restaurant managers thought and worked, and the help files read like a programmer's debugging tools rather than operations manuals. The problems with the design could easily have been avoided had the power of the advocate for the client on the team been better balanced with that of the development manager.

Example of Project Roles

There's no one right way to define project roles that will apply in every case. What works will vary by specific project environment. But to give you a more concrete idea of what one looks like, here's an example of a particularly well-conceived project structure. The list is derived from the project roles that Microsoft uses on its own internal projects as described in the Microsoft Solutions Framework. When taken collectively, these six generic project roles ensure that the necessary project tasks are completed and the needs of project constituencies are appropriately considered:

- *Project manager.* The project manager views the project through the lens of three major projects constraints: schedule, budget, and features of the technical product. Her goal is to drive the group to define the appropriate balance among the three and ensure that the project is delivered within those constraints. The project manager coordinates information flow, negotiations, and project process. She also drives the definition of the detailed specification of the range of technical features that will be included in the final product. Throughout the project, she tracks and reports status and is the advocate for the project constraints.
- *Client advocate.* The client advocate views the project through the lens of customer satisfaction. His goal is to complete the project with a happy customer. The client advocate serves in a

liaison role between the project team and the client, attempting to synchronize expectations on both sides. To the project team, he acts as the advocate for the client. To the client, he acts as the advocate for the project team. The client advocate ensures that the project team really understands what the client wants and needs for the project to be successful, and he also manages client expectations to keep them realistic. The client advocate is, as the title implies, the advocate for the client.

- *Technical lead.* The technical lead views the project through the lens of the technical product. His goal is to deliver the product according to the specifications within the budgeted time and cost. The technical lead drives the technical design and construction of the solution according to the specifications. He is an advocate for the technical product.

- *Test lead.* The test lead views the project through the lens of status. The goal is to understand the true status of the technical product. The role throughout the project is to constantly determine the functional status of the product through objective tests and share that information with the rest of the team to support fact-based decision making. The test leader is not the adversary of the technical lead but an important information source to the whole team. The test lead is the advocate for the truth.

- *Deployment lead.* The deployment lead views the project through the lens of deployment and support. Her goal is to deploy the technical product and ensure that once installed, it can be supported easily in the user environment. The deployment lead plans and executes the product rollout and is the advocate for the technical operations and support personnel.

- *User experience lead.* The user experience lead views the project through the lens of the system users. As opposed to the client, who pays for the construction of the system, the users are the people who use the system to do their daily jobs. The user experience's goal is to enhance the performance of users, that is, enable them to do their jobs better, faster, and or more cheaply. Her tasks include reviewing the system for usability and developing support materials, such as manuals, help screens, and training classes. User experience is the advocate for the user.

Managing Assignments

Geek leaders answer the second question of task ambiguity, "Who will play each role?" by making assignments, that is, deciding which person will take on each role. Making assignment decisions is one of the most important things that a geek leader does. On the surface, it may seem a simple administrative duty, but in fact, it lies at the very heart of every geek organization and affects almost every facet of its success. In his classic book *Managing the Professional Service Firm*, David Maister devotes an entire chapter to the subject of the importance of scheduling resources. The same importance applies in geek groups.

The activity of managing assignments may seem simple. You take project roles and people, and mix and match them. Multiple people may be assigned to a role, and individual people may be assigned to multiple roles. All you've got to do is make sure that all the roles are covered and that the people in the roles can perform them well. It's that easy—and that complex.

In the making of these assignments, in allocating resources, you shape the organization and the individuals in it in ways that you may not immediately appreciate. In addition, the composition of teams becomes a critical factor in project success. Just throwing together a bunch of random people doesn't usually result in quality projects. You've got to pay much closer attention to the individuals filling the project roles.

This is one of the dangers of the project role concept. Once you've thought through the archetypal roles in abstract, there is a temptation to forget that each person who inhabits a role will interpret it in his or her own way. Just as you would get a very different Hamlet if you cast Sir John Gielgud, the famed Shakespearean actor, as opposed to Steve Martin, the comedian, each person will play a particular role differently. You've got to consider the project team as a whole when trying to build a successful team.

Importance of Resource Allocation

When you choose who will be assigned to which role on a project, you are making seemingly small decisions that have consequences that accumulate to significant proportions. Although any one decision may not make or break a project or department, a few key decisions can have significant effects:

- *Team success.* Although many factors can affect whether a project is ultimately successful, the most common killers of projects are all related to communication and human infrastructure. Projects that fail don't usually fail due to problems with technology. They fail due to poor team communication, inflexible processes, team infighting, and lack of business-technology alignment.
- *Staff motivation.* A number of the primary motivational factors for geeks can be traced directly to which projects they are assigned. If you assign people who are interested in a project from the outset, you've already gone a long way toward ensuring that the team is motivated to perform.
- *Customer service quality.* Customer service quality can also be directly tied to team construction. If you assign people who are not motivated by the project, the technology, the role, or the team, you are unlikely to have people dedicated to top-notch customer service.
- *Employee retention.* Geeks are highly valuable and mobile. Generally, they are more loyal to their technology than to a company, so are subject to high turnover. They also tend to have little patience for projects that don't interest them. If they have too many assignments in a row that they view as bad, most will start looking for a new job.
- *Employee training.* Every project brings training opportunities for those assigned to the project. Whether you assign them to learn

by filling a new project role, a new technology, or a new business function, if they are learning, they are more likely to be happy and become more valuable to the company at the same time.

- *Employee career path.* Each project brings opportunities to change the career direction for individuals assigned to the project. Each assignment brings the opportunity to fulfill or dash the career aspirations of geeks in your group. A programmer may start out on the road to becoming a manager. A technical writer may start the transition into testing. A deployment specialist may become a programmer.

- *Project cost.* Assignments have substantial effects on direct project costs. Since the salaries of individuals vary widely, an assignment choice can save or blow a budget.

- *Departmental efficiency.* Assignments have a direct relationship to overall departmental efficiency. If you don't keep everyone committed to projects, then you are paying people who are not assigned to productive work. Although all people need some downtime for study to hone their skills as well as personal time off, few leaders can afford to have hordes of people on the payroll who are not doing productive work.

Building Effective Teams

I've developed a model to help make some sense out of what a well-structured team looks like. It's described by a two-dimensional chart (see Figure 11.1) that's self-promotionally named after my consulting company, C2 Consulting.

The C2 Skills Framework, originally designed to help clients with technical team problems, has proven to be a useful tool in analyzing work teams, making assignments, diagnosing team performance issues, and prescribing corrective action. (I will present only part of it here, since the details get more into the particulars of project management than would be appropriate for this book.)

The framework describes and categorizes the types of skills that individuals and teams need to complete technical projects

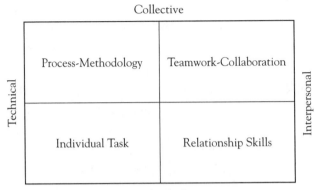

FIGURE 11.1. The C2 Skills Framework.

successfully. It contrasts skills on two independent scales and then classifies them into one of four categories.

The first scale is the Technical–Interpersonal scale. On one end of the scale are the purely technical skills, that is, the ability to apply specialized professional knowledge to technical or managerial problems—for example, the ability to apply the knowledge of a variety of functional specialties to information technology, project management, finance, marketing, testing, or technical writing. Technical skills help you do the tasks of your job. On the other end of the scale are interpersonal skills—generic skills related to building and maintaining productive relationships with other people in the work environment.

The second scale is the Individual–Collective scale. On one end of this scale are the individual skills, which are the ones that help you be personally productive, that help you work alone, or to get what you need from other individuals to complete your work. At the other end of the scale are the collective skills, which help you work in larger group contexts.

When you cross these two independent axes, you get four quadrants that describe categories of skills:

- Individual–Technical (individual task skills)
- Collective–Technical (process or methodology skills)
- Individual–Interpersonal (relationship skills)
- Collective–Interpersonal (teamwork or collaboration skills)

Individual Task Skills. These skills allow you to become personally productive in the field of your specialty. For example, a programmer's individual task skills might include the ability to design, code, unit test, and debug programs in a variety of environments and languages. A project manager's individual task skills might include the ability to structure projects, build and manage plans, or write status reports in a manner that is useful to managers and clients. A test lead's individual task skills might include test planning, test execution, test result tracking, or bug tracking and reporting.

In short, individual task skills are those that allow you to do the work that you produce with your own hands. For every job, every functional specialty, no matter how managerial, there are certain things you produce yourself. Whether you code programs, write documents and reports, write performance reviews, or circulate agendas, you must produce some sort of artifact or deliverable. Whatever skills it takes for you be productive in your specialty are your individual task skills.

Most geeks spend their entire academic career focused on acquiring individual task skills, such as learning programming languages, data structures, and analysis techniques. And it's these skills that they often believe are most important. In fact, many geeks don't even think about any other types of skills.

Unfortunately, most resource allocation managers think about only these too, as if just having a group of people with the right mix of technical skills were sufficient to complete a project successfully. It's not.

Process-Methodology Skills. Process-methodology skills constitute those that you need to help a group of people work together on a technical problem and be productive individually and collectively. These skills typically include things like being able to break apart a big problem into many smaller ones that can be handled by individuals or smaller subgroups, assigning the tasks, planning projects and accounting for interdependencies, and properly sequencing tasks so that the big problem is solved at the end. In other words, can you handle the mechanics of making a group project run? These are still technical skills, focused purely on productively completing tasks.

Relationship Skills. These skills allow you to form and maintain a one-on-one professional relationship with another person in which each of you gets what you need from the other to be productive. Relationship skills typically include verbal communication, active and passive listening, basic negotiations, written communication, building trust, and emotional intelligence. In other words, can you work one-on-one with another person productively without causing nasty fights or hard feelings to develop?

Teamwork-Collaboration Skills. Teamwork-collaboration skills are those that allow you to work productively in a group setting. They go beyond those of relationship skills. Teamwork skills typically include group conversation give and take, coalition building, group negotiations, listening, meeting management, political skills, verbal communication in a group setting, facilitation, building group trust, and written communications. These skills help everyone to be productive in a group setting.

Balancing Teams. Teams that I find to be most successful are those that combine an appropriate balance of all four categories of skills. Few individuals are exceptional in all four categories. Each person brings a balance of skills and deficits in each of the areas. But as a whole, groups that are collectively unbalanced tend to have a difficult time completing projects successfully.

The most common problem is the team that's composed solely of people who are strong at individual task skills and lack even a basic awareness of the other skills. No matter how capable they are technically, no matter how good-willed they may be, without the ability to balance the technical skills with the other three, projects eventually break down. The team members don't know how to solve problems collectively, only individually, so the project begins to fall apart on the technical end or the interpersonal end.

Another common problem comes up when a team is too focused on process-methodology skills and lacks strength in other areas (especially technical individual tasks). These groups become obsessed with planning the project in such detail that they never actually do the project.

When constructing a team, it is helpful to assess the strengths and weaknesses of each potential team member in each of these quadrants. Then look at possible groupings of individuals who will make up the teams and determine how their skills complement one another. If you assign a reasonably balanced group without any single individuals who are wildly out of kilter with others on the team, your project is more likely to succeed.

Making Judgments

The final question of task ambiguity, "What are the prerogatives of geek leaders, and how are they exercised?" brings us back to the questions of leadership and power. On a day-to-day task level, what judgments do leaders need to make? Where can they and should they step in to make explicit decisions for geeks?

As should already be clear, it's best to let the project teams themselves resolve their own issues, but occasionally, you've got to step in and do it for them. Sometimes there's no time for consensus building. Sometimes situations involve legal liability. Occasionally, a team descends into groupthink, where no one is willing to speak up for common sense.

Often these judgments are about setting standards for what's expected. Occasionally, groups settle for the least common denominator and are willing to deliver something that doesn't meet the standards of the leader's vision for the organization. This is where you mold the expectations of the group for product, process, behavior, and culture. It doesn't mean that you must be an ogre, but the job of the leader is to demonstrate expectations by making explicit judgments about people, product, or behavior.

The better you are at leading geeks, the rarer these circumstances should be, but they will arise at least occasionally.

Defining Done

One of the most subtle and difficult issues for project teams is to declare a project over and a product complete. Without the physical reality that governs most types of work, knowing what is done can be quite difficult and require careful negotiation among all of the constituencies of a project.

Sometimes project teams carry on too long, sacrificing schedule and budget in favor of an unattainable level of quality, or they wait for some nonessential part of the system to be completed. In these cases, they may need prodding to remind them of the priorities of the project and what decisions might best serve the needs of the clients.

Sometimes project teams declare victory too soon, only to deliver a nonfunctional product that lacks the necessary functionality, stability, or quality. Similarly, in these cases, you may need to step in to urge the team forward.

On the fast food restaurant management system project that I described earlier in the chapter, we ran into this problem too. The development manager, who was in charge of the whole project, declared that the system was ready for deployment much sooner than the rest of us felt was appropriate. The software had been written, and it did do what the developers set out to do. But not only did it do in a way that the users would never understand, it was way too slow. It took more than twenty minutes from the time the program was launched until the first screen appeared. The development manager's reasoning was that the business would only have to launch the program once a day, so he considered it acceptable to wait twenty minutes. He felt that employees should just do something else while the program was loading. Despite his assurances, the rest of us didn't consider the system quite ready to go. His interpretation of *done* didn't match that of the rest of the management team (and he continued to disagree with the rest of us until the day he was fired).

Delineating Quality

This is a special case of defining done. Although it's best for the project team to define that for themselves, sometimes it's not possible. Occasionally, a project sets out to create something totally new—not a replacement for an existing system, not a slightly improved product to compete in an existing market, but something that has no precedent. Often, these types of products don't even have clearly defined marketplaces as they are designed.

In these situations, it's not easy to let the advocacy system determine what an acceptable product is, since it's not entirely clear whom the advocates are representing. Although the theory of marketing says that you've got to identify a customer and a need before beginning product development, this isn't always the case in the real world of high technology.

When Apple Computer was designing the first Macintosh, it wasn't entirely clear who would use the system. And although there were a number of incredibly talented software developers on that team with opinions about how the system should work, they had no objective basis on which to make decisions about the look and feel of the product. Other than the experimental Alto system that they had seen at Xerox, there was no precedent. Steve Jobs,

Apple's charismatic founder and Macintosh team leader, became well known for his tirades over work that he considered to be of unacceptable quality. Although his opinions were not necessarily delivered in the most productive manner, it was important that he make judgments about quality, since there were no easy answers about the right way to build the product.

Circumscribing Acceptable Behavior

On occasion, geek groups can be rather adolescent and rambunctious in nature, and generally that's just fine. But sometimes enthusiasm gets out of hand, or occasionally under the influence of a strong personality, a group begins to develop characteristics that are simply unacceptable. In these cases, you as the leader have to put your foot down and define clearly the boundaries of acceptable behavior. Sometimes you'll have to call in a behavioral consultant to help the group accept the limits.

Sometimes a general incivility grows up in a group as factions form around positions or projects. This can be quite difficult to root out, but if the environment becomes unsafe for sharing ideas, you begin to lose the intellectual content in your intellectual property, not to mention that it becomes an unpleasant place to work.

Sometimes behavior can become a legal liability. If casual fun starts to blur the lines of harassment, it's time to put a stop to it, quickly and forcefully. Not only is it the right thing to do ethically, it's also good risk management.

You as a leader retain responsibility for judging the boundaries of acceptable behavior.

Rewarding Outstanding Performance

The most common form of judgment comes in rewarding performance. Whether handing out bonuses, prizes, compliments, or recognition, it falls to the leader to judge the value of individual or group contributions to the organization.

Geeks are very sensitive about performance measurement, reviews, and rewards, as are most other employees. But it's here that geeks' strong belief in meritocracy comes into full bloom. Generally, geeks prefer that reviews and rewards be based on objective, measurable standards. They also generally prefer that those standards be based solely on technical knowledge and perhaps delivery.

Unfortunately, the demands for objective, measurable performance standards cannot always be easily met. Performing geekwork entails many levels of subtle contribution, only one of which is purely technical. You, as a leader, must define what constitutes good and outstanding performance and strive to communicate your expectations. Then you must reward those who consistently meet or exceed them. It is a fundamental leadership function that helps clarify task ambiguity.

Punishing Poor Performance

Just as you must issue judgments about outstanding performers, you must also identify, correct, and ultimately punish poor performance. Unfortunately, the negative role comes with the positive one. You can't spend all of your time just handing out awards, since not all geeks are top performers. It's part of the life of leadership. As you provide judgment about performance, you must also follow up on unacceptable performance too.

Tips for Managing Task Ambiguity

Here are a few thoughts on effectively managing task ambiguity:

- *Design roles independently from assignments.* It's very easy to start thinking about a project based first on which geeks are or could be made available. Generally, it's a mistake to start off that way. A better way is to think about the play before casting the actors. You can always modify the roles once you know who will be in the cast.

- *When you modify roles due to assignments, make sure that the roles still work.* Whenever you make changes to project roles because of the individuals whom you assign to the roles, review whether the roles still fulfill the criteria for an effective work structure.

- *Acknowledge the knowledge inversion.* Be honest with yourself and others on the team about the distribution of specialist knowledge on a project. No one individual, superior or subordinate, knows everything about the business, technology, and organization. You shouldn't feel that you need to know it all, but neither should you accept that technologists do either.

- *Make judgments in bursts.* When you do have to make explicit decisions that are enforced through power, get as many of them out of the way as you can at one time. If you drip out decisions every few hours, you'll become known as a controlling manager. If you make the same number of decisions but hand them out only once a week, your reputation will be quite different.

Summary

FUNDAMENTAL QUESTIONS

- How do geek leaders manage task ambiguity?
- What are project roles, and how do they help geeks be productive?
- What are assignments, and why are they important?
- What are judgments, and how do they help geeks be productive?

KEY IDEAS

- Task ambiguity encompasses three questions: Who are the characters in the story of a project? Who will play each role? and What are the prerogatives of geek leaders, and how are they exercised?

- Once projects have been selected and processes defined, geek leaders define the roles that must be played within a project and test these roles against a number of important criteria to ensure that they make sense.

- Geek leaders assign individuals to fill roles. When assigning individuals to roles, it's very important to consider much more than the technical skills required to complete project tasks. Team success is based on a balance of four skill sets described in the C2 Skills Framework.

- The final role that a leader plays in resolving task ambiguity is that of judge. Ultimately, a leader must take responsibility for helping to clarify when projects are really finished, what an acceptable product is, what acceptable behavior is for geeks, how well each individual performed, and what rewards and punishments should be granted based on performance.

CONCLUSION

Harmonizing Context and Content

12

How Geek Leaders Lead

Now that we've covered all of the elements of the context and content of geek leadership, there's only one more question to explore: How do geek leaders lead? The answer is that they seek to harmonize the content and context of geekwork. They strive to build coherence among the environment, the work, the culture, and the approaches to geekwork.

Of course, as in most other ambiguous knowledge work, each answer brings its own questions. Again, the question is, How? How do they harmonize the content and context of geekwork? The answers have already been provided in a number of chapters but are worthy of highlight here. First, geek leaders bring coherence to the workplace through the stories they tell—the narratives that hold together the chaotic world of geekwork. And second, they use themselves, their embodiments of their narratives, to verify the truth of their stories.

Harmonizing Content and Context

Geekwork is anchored by its inherent ambiguity—its consistent uncertainty and inconsistent facts. Contradictions and paradox are just a regular part of the business. The ultimate goal for leaders in this environment is to fight against doubt and dissonance, to harmonize the content and context of geek leadership. Although it may be an unattainable goal, it is the striving that transforms unorganized, unproductive, unhappy groups into focused, driven, goal-oriented ones.

As sense-making animals, humans in general, and geeks in particular, have a strong need for order and consistency. In part, it's why the problem-solution thinking model is so compelling for them. Every action, every thought is focused on answering questions, pushing back the frontiers of chaos, and expanding the bubble of clarity, knowledge, and consistency.

This need extends beyond a simple desire for consistency. It is part of the deep-seated emotional needs that lie at the core of humanity's drive for knowledge, understanding, and dominance over the environment. Although geeks' passion for reason may lead them to focus more on the conceptual and cognitive aspects of harmony, the need is ultimately an emotional one.

Harmonizing content and context does more than manage ambiguity. In managing ambiguity, geek leaders help to answer fundamental questions about environment, structure, and tasks; in harmonizing, they seek to align the disparate answers for internal coherence and completeness. For example, when the leaders of a small technology company interpret its environment, recognizing that it has ten employees versus the fifty thousand of its largest competitor yet insisting that it provide the same range of products and services, they are attempting to create an unrealistic, grandiose identity that is inconsistent with the interpretation of the market. Harmonizing might force them to consider on which limited range of products and services the company may reasonably compete and to forge a more reasonable identity for the group.

In addition, leaders must harmonize the approach to answering the questions and performing work with the answers themselves. For example, it's very difficult for a leader to declare dictatorially that all workers feel empowered. More than a humorous irony, the means of leadership can easily undermine the ends of a leader who lacks a sense of harmony.

Inconsistencies in the answers to fundamental questions or con-flicts between the actions of leaders and the answers to questions at best undermine the clarity that geeks strive for and at worst may be perceived as hypocrisy on the part of a leader. Either interpretation saps motivation and limits the effectiveness of geekwork.

The Tools of Leadership: Narrative and Embodiment

Leaders have two key tools at their disposal in harmonizing context and content. They're the same tools of leadership that religious and social leaders have used since the beginning of time to win over the hearts and minds of populations. In his groundbreaking book *Leading Minds: An Anatomy of Leadership*, Harvard psychologist Howard Gardner identifies the centrality of the stories leaders tell and their embodiment of those stories to effective leadership.

Narratives speak to the deepest longings and often unspoken needs of humanity. They seem to be wired somehow in the human brain, as the craving for stories seems to begin early in life. As chil-dren acquire language, they simultaneously begin constructing and consuming stories. Child's play centers on creating narratives such as stories and games.

As children become adults, their relationship with narratives grows and changes but never diminishes. As self-awareness grows, identity develops, and worldviews form, narratives remain impor-tant as development raises a constant stream of new questions to be explored.

Within all realms of life, whenever we try to make sense of the complex and contradictory environment, we turn to narratives—stories to knit together and bring meaning to the complex and dis-parate facts of the world. Faced with the most profound mysteries of existence, of identity and purpose, of meaning, morality, and mor-tality, we seek out narratives as comprehensive, comprehensible vessels to bundle together and hold important questions, observable facts, unsolvable problems, and paradoxes in a coherent form. It's no coincidence that religions are based on a core set of stories that seek to answer the central questions of life. "Who are we?" "Where did we come from?" "Why are we here?" "What is our relationship with the rest of the observable universe?" Every nation writes and reinterprets the story of its history, of its founding, the identity of its people, and its purpose. And every technology organization does the same thing on a much smaller scale.

The narratives that a leader provides or adopts knit together the facts of an organization's existence—an interpretation of its environment, purpose, identity, and strategy. And just as there are many religions that interpret the mysteries of human life through different stories, an organization can define its core stories in many ways.

The term *narrative* is used here in its broadest sense to include more than myths, movies, fairy tales, and novels—to encompass almost any coherent simplification and representation of events, ideas, and characters. More than just traditional stories, they include many other forms of sense making, such as models, theories, plans, and projections.

The second tool leaders have at their disposal is that of embodiment. As leaders craft and select stories to bring form and order to followers' ideas about the organization, their actions may either embody or contradict the interpretations and values promoted in the stories. Leaders embody their stories when they display behavior that is consistent with and reinforces the messages of their narratives. To embody their stories, leaders must not only act consistently with the values expressed in their narratives, but must do so in an authentic rather than a forced manner. Artificial or forced behavior does not validate a leader's stories. Geeks are particularly sensitive about issues of embodiment and can easily dismiss a leader perceived as a hypocrite or a faker.

Together, narratives and embodiments represent the primary symbols through which leaders lead. Narratives are the primary tools for managing ambiguity and influencing followers, peers, superiors, customers, partners, and others. Leaders themselves also serve as a symbol through the embodiment of their narratives.

Collectively, the narratives either mutually reinforce or undermine each other.

Subjects of Narratives

Leaders lead through a variety of narratives that bring coherence to a group. There is no one simple story that can encapsulate all of the information needed to lead a group. Over time, small narratives cluster together to become conglomerations, much as scenes cluster into acts and acts into plays. In addition, a leader's narratives encompass a wide range of subjects, each with a purpose and place in the constellation of ideas that help resolve ambiguity.

A geek leader's narratives usually include stories about the following subjects:

- *The context of geek leadership.* Stories are the way that leaders interpret and communicate about the sociopolitical environment, the organization, geeks, leaders, and geekwork.
- *The content of geek leadership.* Internal coordination is performed through the intricate creation and exchange of narratives such as plans and documents. External representation is done through the expression and exchange of the narratives of the group. Similarly, motivation is nurtured and ambiguity managed through narratives.
- *Leaders.* Leaders offer narratives about themselves, their history, and their relationship with the organization and followers. These stories represent a critical part of the bonding between leaders and followers, communicating information about expertise, legitimacy, values, and vision.
- *Geeks.* Leaders tell stories about their followers—their triumphs, failures, and relationships. These stories are also critical to forming the bond between leaders and followers, offering information about the identity of geeks and how a leader views followers.
- *Past, present, and future.* Leaders interpret and communicate about the past and present of a market, an organization, a group, or

an individual through the use of narratives. Similarly, they project the future in narrative form as well.

- *Values*. Every story expresses values, judgments about right and wrong, good and evil, and priorities. Some are explicit, while others are subtler. Some are deliberately included in narratives, while others are unintended expressions of hidden or even subconscious motivations.

Functions of Narrative and Embodiment

Together, a leader's narratives contribute to the formation of world-views of both leaders and geeks. When they serve to harmonize content and context, they support all of the responsibilities of geek leadership. When they conflict with one another, the dissonance distracts attention from geekwork and diminishes effectiveness in creating technology that supports the overall goals of the group.

Narrative, Embodiment, and Motivation. Narrative is among a leader's most potent tools in attempting to nurture motivation among geeks. The power of narrative to help answer some of the most fundamental questions for both groups and individuals helps leaders create an environment in which intrinsic motivation for creativity flourishes.

A narrative defines for an organization, department, or project team the sense of identity answering the "Who are we?" question that so often bedevils groups. This definition helps to establish the boundaries that define membership and relationships with outsiders, and it can even hint at the purpose of a group's existence.

In fact, if you reexamine the foundation for the geekwork model discussed in Chapter Nine, it will become clear that it is really a structured way of viewing the narratives that leaders and followers develop to support their work. Leaders tell stories to frame issues, interpret the environment, and define purpose, laying the foundation for motivation to develop. Each follower develops his or her individual narratives of identity and meaning, interpreting and evaluating the leader's stories.

Motivation is particularly sensitive to issues of embodiment. When a leader displays consistency between narratives and behavior, the ideas and information of the narratives are validated, and motivation can develop. Inconsistency calls both the content of a leader's narratives and the integrity of the leader into question, creating, at best, a distraction and, at worst, a mutiny.

Narrative, Embodiment, and Representation. Coherent and compelling narratives provide a foundation for furnishing external representation. In addition to establishing group identity and boundaries, which are clearly needed to identify external entities, narratives also serve to undergird the relationships established between the leader and outside groups.

Not only do narratives provide information to group members about their identity, but they also communicate that same information to outsiders, who also need to understand who geeks are, what they do, and how they relate to the rest of the organization. Narratives also help outsiders develop their own measures of meaning and significance for geekwork and technology.

The narratives need to prove compelling not only to the geeks within a group but to outsiders, including upward executive management, peer organizations, customers, and partners. If the narratives are compelling only to geeks, a leader will have trouble establishing support, acquiring resources, and even getting attention from senior management.

And just as with motivation, narratives are most effective when the leader embodies their values and ideas.

Narrative, Embodiment, and Facilitation. Narrative provides information to geeks about the internal structure of the group, the roles of leader and followers, and the values and culture that the group aspires to.

Powerful and compelling narratives reduce the need for internal facilitation. When all the geeks in a group understand the purpose of the group, the roles they play, how they are expected to interact with one another, and how they should coordinate with one another, less of the burden of coordination falls on the leader as an individual and is distributed more effectively across the group.

When geeks buy into the group's narratives, the tension that can develop between leaders and followers over issues of control is reduced. The more committed that individuals in the group are to the values and goals of the narratives, the less a leader needs to be directive. A leader will then be more likely viewed as a facilitator helping a group reach its goals rather than a powerful overseer to resist.

Narrative, Embodiment, and Ambiguity. More than anything else, narrative is the tool for resolving ambiguity at all three levels of the hierarchy. As one of the most important tools humans have for helping to make sense of the world, narratives are the response to ambiguity. Stories transform chaotic facts and observations into coherent patterns that we can comprehend and retain with relative ease.

You can think of the hierarchy of ambiguity as a system for classifying narratives that need to be developed in order to create an effective organization. Each layer of the hierarchy poses questions and issues that need to be responded to in the form of narratives that sufficiently resolve the issues and provide both the factual information and the emotional content to drive an organization.

Vital Narratives

Among the many narratives that leaders develop and tell, not all have the same importance to a group. Some are merely for entertainment and bonding. Others provide some minor information but nothing crucial. But there are two narratives that play a particularly prominent role in forging an effective organization: the defining narrative and the leader's vision for the future of the organization.

The defining narrative provides the conceptual and emotional foundation for establishing group identity. It usually consists of the history of the organization or group, combined with an interpretation of elements of the context of geek leadership. Together, these ideas form one of the most important core stories to help a group make sense of the reason for its existence and its relationship with the outside world.

The defining narrative for Apple Computer, for example, has grown to become an industry legend. In April 1976, two computer hobbyists, Steve Wozniak, age twenty-five, and Steve Jobs, age twenty-one, started out to sell microcomputers that they assembled in Jobs's parents' garage. The Apple I was a modest success and quickly led to the Apple II, which became a blockbuster. Wozniak and Jobs's original purpose was to make computers for geeks, but by the time they introduced the Macintosh, Apple's story was complete. Until that time, all computers were hard to use and expensive. Apple's new purpose was to make computers that were so easy to use that they would be in every household. Even this brief telling of the story hints at the elements of its technical engineering culture, aesthetic approach, and points of differentiation from others in the market.

The leader's vision for a group builds on the defining narrative and projects it out into the future. It describes both a view of the defining narrative of the group at some future time and the transformational path between the current state and the future state.

To help geeks be effective, the defining narrative and vision together should:

- Define a high-level strategy for overcoming obstacles in achieving the future state.
- Link geeks and geekwork with the future state.
- Identify or imply organizational values.
- Outline a quest worth pursuing.

Evolution of Narratives

Although building and maintaining narratives is one of the key tools that leaders use to lead, it would be a mistake to believe that developing and communicating narratives is the sole province of leaders. In this age of free-flowing information and especially when working with geeks, new narratives, additions to old ones, and modifications to existing ones can come from anywhere and anyone.

Although you may have a particular interpretation or projection of some facet of the external environment like the marketplace, an article in the morning *Wall Street Journal* could easily challenge your view and destabilize your previously accepted narrative interpreting the marketplace. You might hire a new middle manager from a competitor who brings along a completely different interpretation of the basis of competition in the market that catches on quickly with the geeks in his group.

As new information emerges and people join and leave the organization, narratives evolve and change. Many of these changes may not be under the control of a particular leader. In fact, at times, a leader's version may be the most difficult one for geeks to accept if they believe that is only a representation of the corporate party line.

Within an organization, the generally accepted version of key narratives is constantly in flux, the result of an almost Darwinian struggle between competing stories that attempt to answer the same questions and interpret the same facts. Which versions of the narrative survive and which are shunted aside can be difficult to predict since there are no generally accepted criteria for what will catch on. Although one version may better fit the facts, another may be more emotionally compelling. Or perhaps the narrative that a leader proposes may best fit the circumstances but be discredited because the leader fails to embody the values of the narrative and the story is dismissed by association.

In addition to directly conflicting or contradicting narratives, new and more complex ones may emerge that subsume older ones.

Just as in physics, new theories frequently explain a broader range of phenomena than older theories and subsume less general ones.

In fact, not only are the creation, communication, and embodiment of compelling and comprehensive narratives not restricted to leaders, they are also an important route to achieving leadership status. Those who comprehend, explain, and plan for increasing levels of ambiguity are often the ones promoted to leadership positions.

As important stories compete for attention within an organization and the prevailing accepted versions change, major disruptions can take place. If a board of directors decides that a CEO's vision is not in harmony with their interpretation of the environment, he may lose his job and be replaced by one whose vision is supported by the board. On a smaller scale, a leader's vision or defining narrative may be rejected by geeks in favor of an opposing one, forcing the leader to change his story or risk losing support.

Building Trust, Respect, and Unity:
The Effects of Narrative and Embodiment

This book closes with a topic that many leadership books start out with: building trust, respect, and unity. You may have noticed the conspicuous absence of a subject of such importance to leaders, but it has been deliberate. Geek leaders who set out with an explicit goal of building trust and respect for themselves frequently fail to acquire it. The formulaic and forced behavior that often accompanies a leader's attempt to build credibility undermines the authenticity of his embodiment of his narratives.

Although the reasoning may seem a bit circular, if you start out to build trust and respect so that you can be an effective leader, you're unlikely to get it. But if you set out to be an effective leader and consistently and authentically work to do so, trust and respect will follow, enabling you to be effective.

Earning the respect of geeks is critical to being an effective leader but can be very difficult. There's a reason that the comic strip

Dilbert, with its depiction of the pointy-haired, incompetent boss, is so popular. Geeks' independence combines with their tendency to make swift and merciless judgments of leaders to make it difficult to earn their respect. Things can be especially tough for leaders without a technical background, since geeks place a high value on technical prowess as a qualification for leadership.

In large measure, respect develops in response to the narratives of a leader. The more comprehensive, coherent, and compelling his stories are, the more he attracts respect for having insight and vision. The more widely communicated, universally accepted, and stable his narratives are, the more he becomes a respected source of information and ideas.

Establishing unity within a geek group also results in large measure in response to a leader's narratives. If they become generally accepted and prove emotionally compelling, followers will unite around the common vision. Unity is ultimately achieved through a group of people independently committing to a single story that brings together elements of identity, purpose, and direction.

Trust is not the same as respect or unity. Geeks may respect the skills and insight of a leader but distrust his motives. Or they may trust his intentions yet not respect his skills and stories. Trust and respect are two independent reactions.

Earning the trust of a group of geeks can be just as difficult as earning their respect, if not more so. Trust carries a more emotional commitment and is given more slowly than respect. A geek group may learn to respect a new leader very quickly as she displays vast knowledge and skill in initial meetings. Trust takes longer to develop and stems largely from the authenticity and consistency with which a leader embodies her stories. If, over an extended period, a leader is judged by geeks to be relatively consistent in her stories and behaves in concert with them, she will be more likely to win their trust. Should she be perceived as self-contradictory or hypocritical, geeks will withhold or remove their trust.

In geek groups, the essential trust and respect that leaders need cannot be sought but only granted.

Summary

FUNDAMENTAL QUESTIONS

- How do geek leaders lead?
- How do geek leaders harmonize content and context?
- How do narratives and embodiments support geek leadership?
- What vital narratives do geek leaders use to guide followers?
- How do geek leaders gain the trust and respect of geeks?

KEY IDEAS

- Geek leaders are most effective when they seek to harmonize the content and context of geek leadership.
- Leaders have two key tools at their disposal to help harmonize content and context: narrative and embodiment.
- Narratives are a geek leader's primary way of communicating about the context and content of geek leadership.
- Stories about content and context that are mutually consistent and compelling support leaders in fulfilling all of their responsibilities.
- Two of the most important narratives that geek leaders develop and communicate are defining narrative, which helps describe and define identity and purpose, and vision, which projects the defining narrative into the future.
- Geek leaders earn the respect of geeks by telling compelling stories of coherence and consistency.
- Geek leaders earn the trust of geeks by consistently embodying the ideas and values of their stories.

Appendix: Models and Lists

This Appendix provides a few of the key lists and the diagrams of the important models that have organized this book.

The Context of Geek Leadership

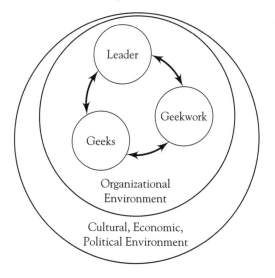

The Content of Geek Leadership

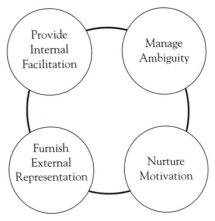

The Hierarchy of Ambiguity

The Foundation for Geekwork

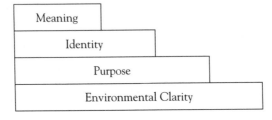

The C2 Skills Framework

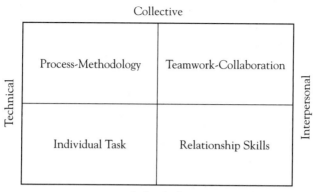

The Nature of Geekwork

- Failure is normal.
- Ambiguity rules.
- Figuring out what to do can be harder than doing it.
- Geekwork is organized by what you don't know.
- Deep concentration.
- What is work?
- Subordinates know more than managers.
- My work, our work.
- The problem with problems.
- Done is hard to do.
- You can't control creativity.
- Estimates are always wrong.

Performing Geekwork: The Twelve Competencies

1. Technical competence
2. Personal productivity
3. Ability to juggle multiple tasks simultaneously
4. Ability to describe the business context of technical work
5. Ability to forge compromises between business and technical constraints
6. Ability to manage client relationships
7. Ability to manage technical teams
8. Ability to play positive politics
9. Ability to help expand client relationships
10. Ability to work through others, to make others productive
11. Ability to manage ambiguity
12. Ability to manage time horizons

Ways to Motivate Geeks

1. Select wisely.
2. Manage meaning.
3. Communicate significance.
4. Show a career path.
5. Projectize.
6. Encourage isolation.
7. Engender external competition.
8. Design interdependence.
9. Limit group size.
10. Control resource availability.
11. Offer free food . . . intermittently.

Ways to Demotivate Geeks

1. Exclusion from decision making
2. Inconsistency
3. Excessive monitoring
4. Focus on tasks, not goals
5. Unqualified evaluation
6. Misaligned extrinsic motivators
7. Artificial deadlines
8. Changing deadlines
9. Organizational disinterest
10. Teams without skills

Functions of External Representation

- Acquiring information
- Establishing and maintaining alignment
- Obtaining resources
- Managing expectations
- Projecting prominence
- Protecting geeks
- Insulating geeks
- Attracting geeks

Notes

Chapter Two

1. If you want to read more about the nature of geeks, consult the References. Gerald Weinberg has long been the pioneer in writing about the human element of technical work. His books have stood the test of time. Even the ones that were written decades ago are just as relevant today as they were when he wrote them.

2. For the two people reading this book who are not familiar with *Star Trek*, it was a science fiction television series from the 1960s that has attained cult status, especially among geeks. Mr. Spock, first officer on the starship *Enterprise,* was a Vulcan, a race of beings that had evolved to so revere logic as to suppress their emotions completely in order to govern their lives by logic.

3. Csikszentmihalyi, M. *Finding Flow.* New York: Basic Books, 1997, pp. 31–32.

4. *Encyclopaedia Britannica.* (15th ed.) 1991, vol. 16, p. 623.

Chapter Four

1. The Standish Group. *Chaos: A Recipe for Success.* Web-based report, 1999.

Chapter Six

1. Amabile, T. "The Motivation for Creativity in Organizations." Harvard Business School Note, 1996, p. 3. Publication no. 9-396-240.

Chapter Seven

1. Hill, L. "Managing Your Team." Harvard Business School Note, 1994, p. 3. Publication no. 9-494-081.

References

Here are a few of my favorite articles and books on subjects related to leading geeks, loosely grouped by topic.

Geeks

Csikszentmihalyi, M. *Finding Flow: The Psychology of Engagement with Everyday Life*. New York: Basic Books, 1997.

Hohmann, L. *Journey of the Software Professional*. Upper Saddle River, N.J.: Prentice Hall, 1996.

Freedman, R. *The IT Consultant: A Commonsense Framework for Managing the Client Relationship*. San Francisco: Jossey-Bass, 2000.

Maister, D. H. *True Professionalism: The Courage to Care About Your People, Your Clients, and Your Career*. New York: Free Press, 1997.

McConnel, S. *After the Gold Rush: Creating a True Profession of Software Engineering*. Redmond, Wash.: Microsoft Press, 1999.

Weinberg, G. M. *The Psychology of Computer Programming*. New York: Van Nostrand Reinhold, 1971.

Weinberg, G. M. *Understanding the Professional Programmer*. New York: Little, Brown, 1982.

Yourdon, E. *Rise and Resurrection of the American Programmer*. Upper Saddle River, N.J.: Yourdon Press, 1996.

Projects and Teams

Katzenbach, J. R., and Smith, D. K. "The Discipline of Teams." *Harvard Business Review*, Mar.-Apr. 1993, pp. 111–120.

Lipman-Blumen, J., and Leavitt, H. J. *Hot Groups: Seeding Them, Feeding Them, and Using Them to Ignite Your Organization*. New York: Oxford University Press, 1999.

McConnell, S. *Code Complete: A Practical Handbook of Software Construction*. Redmond, Wash.: Microsoft Press, 1993.

Peters, T. *The Project 50 (Reinventing Work): Fifty Ways to Transform Every "Task" into a Project That Matters!* New York: Random House, 1999.

Technical Management

Brooks, F. P., Jr. *The Mythical Man-Month: Essays on Software Engineering*. Reading, Mass.: Addison-Wesley, 1975.

Cusumano, M. A., and Selby, R. W. *Microsoft Secrets: How the World's Most Powerful Software Company Creates Technology, Shapes Markets, and Manages People*. New York: Touchstone, 1995.

DeMarco, T. *Why Does Software Cost So Much? And Other Puzzles of the Information Age*. New York: Dorset House, 1995.

Hoch, D. J., and others. *Secrets of Software Success: Management Insights from 100 Software Firms Around the World*. Boston: Harvard Business School Press, 2000.

McCarthy, J. *Dynamics of Software Development*. Redmond, Wash.: Microsoft Press, 1995.

Standish Group International. *Chaos: A Recipe for Success*. West Yarmouth, Mass.: Standish Group International, 1999.

Weinberg, G. M. *Becoming a Technical Leader: An Organic Problem-Solving Approach*. New York: Dorset House, 1986.

Leadership

Bennis, W. *On Becoming a Leader*. Reading, Mass.: Addison-Wesley, 1989.

Bennis, W., and Biederman, P. W. *Organizing Genius: The Secrets of Creative Collaboration*. Cambridge, Mass.: Perseus, 1997.

Bennis, W., and Nanus, B. *Leaders: The Strategies for Taking Charge*. New York: HarperCollins, 1985.

Burns, J. M. *Leadership*. New York: HarperCollins, 1978.

Gardner, H. *Leading Minds: An Anatomy of Leadership*. New York: Basic Books, 1995.

Gardner, J. W. *On Leadership*. New York: Free Press, 1990.

Schein, E. H. *Organizational Culture and Leadership*. San Francisco: Jossey-Bass, 1992.

Managing Professionals

Humphrey, W. S. *Managing for Innovation: Leading Technical People*. Upper Saddle River, N.J.: Prentice Hall, 1987.

Humphrey, W. S. *Managing Technical People: Innovation, Teamwork, and the Software Process*. Reading, Mass.: Addison-Wesley, 1997.

Ivancevich, J. M., and Duening, T. N. *Managing Einsteins: Leading High-Tech Workers in the Digital Age*. New York: McGraw-Hill, 2002.

Kim, W. C., and Mauborgne, R. "Fair Process: Managing in the Knowledge Economy." *Harvard Business Review*, July-Aug. 1997, pp. 65–75.

Lorsch, J. W., and Mathias, P. F. "When Professionals Have to Manage." *Harvard Business Review*, July-Aug. 1987, pp. 78–83.

Maister, D. H. *Managing the Professional Service Firm*. New York: Free Press, 1993

Mintzberg, H. "Covert Leadership: Notes on Managing Professionals." *Harvard Business Review*, Nov.-Dec. 1998, pp. 140–147.

Morley, E., and Silver, A. "A Film Director's Approach to Managing Creativity." *Harvard Business Review*, Mar.-Apr. 1977, pp. 59–68.

Peters, T. *Professional Service Firm 50: Fifty Ways to Transform Your "Department" into a Professional Service Firm Whose Trademarks are Passion and Innovation!* New York: Random House, 1999.

Pfeffer, J., and Sutton, R. I. "The Smart-Talk Trap." *Harvard Business Review*, May-June 1999, pp. 134–142.

Quinn, J. B., Anderson, P., and Finkelstein, S. "Managing Professional Intellect: Making the Most of the Best." *Harvard Business Review*, Mar.-Apr. 1996, pp. 71–80.

Raelin, J. A. *The Clash of Cultures: Managers Managing Professionals*. Boston: Harvard Business School Press, 1991.

Motivation

Amabile, T. M. "Creativity and Innovation in Organizations." Harvard Business School report, 1996.

Amabile, T. M. "How to Kill Creativity." *Harvard Business Review*, Sept.-Oct. 1998, pp. 76–87.

Amabile, T. M. "Managing for Creativity." Harvard Business School report, 1996.

Amabile, T. M. "The Motivation for Creativity in Organizations." Harvard Business School report, 1996.

Hertzberg, F. "One More Time: How Do You Motivate Employees?" *Harvard Business Review*, Sept.-Oct. 1987, pp. 6–13.

Katzenbach, J. R., and Santamaria, J. A. "Firing Up the Front Line." *Harvard Business Review*, May-June 1999, pp. 107–117.

Kidder, T. *The Soul of a New Machine*. New York: Atlantic-Little, Brown, 1981.

Levinson, H. "Asinine Attitudes Toward Motivation." *Harvard Business Review*, Jan.-Feb. 1973, pp. 70–75.

Stories

Levy, S. *Insanely Great: The Life and Times of Macintosh, the Computer That Changed Everything*. New York: Penguin Books, 1994.

Linzmayer, O. *Apple Confidential: The Real Story of Apple Computer, Inc.* San Francisco: No Starch Press, 1999.

McKee, R. *Story: Substance, Structure, Style, and the Principles of Screenwriting*. New York: ReganBooks, 1997.

The Author

Paul Glen is a principal of C2 Consulting. Since founding the firm in 1999, Glen has been consulting, writing, and speaking about building effective technology organizations. For more than fifteen years, he has advised clients in North America, Europe, and Asia. He has also served as an adjunct faculty member in the M.B.A. programs at the University of Southern California's Marshall School of Business and Loyola Marymount University in Los Angeles. Prior to founding C2 Consulting, he was western regional manager for SEI Information Technology, a national IT consultancy. He holds an M.B.A. from the J. L. Kellogg Graduate School of Management at Northwestern University. And, yes, he is a geek.

Index